Building a Windows NT Internet Server

Eric Harper
Matt Arnett
R. Paul Singh

NRP
NEW RIDERS
PUBLISHING

New Riders Publishing, Indianapolis, Indiana

Building a Windows NT Internet Server

By Eric Harper, Matt Arnett, and R. Paul Singh

Published by:
New Riders Publishing
201 West 103rd Street
Indianapolis, IN 46290 USA

Copyright © 1995 by New Riders Publishing

Printed in the United States of America 1 2 3 4 5 6 7 8 9 0

CIP data available upon request

Warning and Disclaimer

This book is designed to provide information about Windows NT Server. Every effort has been made to make this book as complete and as accurate as possible, but no warranty or fitness is implied.

The information is provided on an "as is" basis. The author and New Riders Publishing shall have neither liability nor responsibility to any person or entity with respect to any loss or damages arising from the information contained in this book or from the use of the disks or programs that may accompany it.

Publisher	Don Fowley
Associate Publisher	Tim Huddleston
Product Development Manager	Rob Tidrow
Marketing Manager	Ray Robinson
Acquisitions Manager	Jim LeValley
Managing Editor	Tad Ringo

Product Development Specialist
Julie Fairweather

Acquisitions Editor
Jim LeValley

Software Specialist
Steve Weiss

Production Editors
Amy Bezek
Stacia Mellinger

Copy Editor
Geneil Breeze

Technical Editor
Rick Fairweather

Assistant Marketing Manager
Tamara Apple

Acquisitions Coordinator
Tracey Turgeson

Publisher's Assistant
Karen Opal

Cover Designer
Nathan Clement

Book Designer
Sandra Schroeder

Production Team Supervisor
Laurie Casey

Graphics Image Specialists
Jason Hand
Clint Lahnen

Production Analysts
Dennis Clay Hager
Angela Bannan,
Bobbi Satterfield
Mary Beth Wakefield

Production Team
Gary Adair, Angela Calvert, Dan Caparo, Nathan Clement, David Garratt, Aleata Howard, Joe Millay, Erika Millen, Beth Rago, Erich J. Richter

Indexer
Bront Davis

About the Authors

Eric Harper is a Reviews Editor for LAN Times Magazine. He works in the LAN Times Testing Center in Provo, Utah, evaluating and writing about Windows, Windows NT, DOS, Unix, and network management products. Before starting at LAN Times, Mr. Harper worked for Novell Technical Support and did some private consulting. He received a B.A. degree from Brigham Young University. His other writing experience includes projects for New Riders, Brady, and Que Publishing.

Matt Flint Arnett is a Product Reviews Editor for LAN Times Magazine. He works in the LAN Times Testing Center in Provo, Utah, where his beats include Internet/online services, optical storage, printing, RAID, security, storage management/tape backup, UPSes, Unix, and virus protection. Matt's background includes analog and digital hardware development and industry listing testing. He also has extensive experience designing Secure Compartmented Information Facilities (SCIF) intruder detection systems for multiple government locations. Just prior to working with LAN Times, Matt owned and operated his own network consulting company in Southern California, where he stressed disaster prevention and data recovery.

R. Paul Singh recently co-founded Internetware, Inc.—a company with a mission to make Internet access easy, secure, and manageable for NetWare LANs. Mr. Singh has been in the networking industry for over 15 years in different engineering and marketing roles. Prior to co-founding Internetware, he had been an independent consultant for two years in the LAN/WAN industry, helping companies develop strategies related to Internet products. Mr. Singh has worked at Telebit Corporation, where he wrote papers and articles on issues related to NetWare IPX protocol in a dial-up environment. Prior to that, he worked at Sun Microsystems, dealing with ISDN and networking issues with multimedia. Mr. Singh also has worked with 3Com Corporation, dealing with third-party relations and product management of network servers. Prior to joining the "vendor world," he worked as a Network Engineer at Morrison Knudsen Engineers. He also has taught computing courses at San Francisco City College.

Mr. Singh has a B.S. in Electrical Engineering form Delhi University, India, and an M.B.A. from St. John's University, New York, specializing in information systems. You can reach him on the Internet at the following address:

pauls@internetware.com

Trademark Acknowledgments

All terms mentioned in this book that are known to be trademarks or service marks have been appropriately capitalized. New Riders Publishing cannot attest to the accuracy of this information. Use of a term in this book should not be regarded as affecting the validity of any trademark or service mark. Windows NT Server is a registered trademark of Microsoft Corporation.

Acknowledgments

From *Eric Harper*: First and foremost, I would like to thank my wonderful wife, Tricia, and my two beautiful children, Lauren and Nathan. Thanks for being so understanding when daddy had to "go to work," even on Saturdays. Thanks for bearing with me through all of the trials, the doubts, the second guesses. Well kids, it's done. Daddy can come out of the Bat Cave now—at least for a little while.

I also would like to thank the great staff at New Riders, especially Julie Fairweather, for helping me steer this book into a form which I hope will be valuable to the readers, for her patient guidance through the latter stages of the project, but most of all for her friendship. Julie, have a *groovy* day.

The author and the publisher of this book wish to thank the European Microsoft Windows NT Academic Centre (EMWAC) for its work in building the tools described in the book and included on the CD-ROM.

EMWAC has been set up to support and act as a focus for Windows NT within academia. It is sponsored by Datalink Computer, Digital, Microsoft, Research Machines, Sequent, and the University of Edinburgh.

From *Matthew Arnett*: As crazy as this year has been (full-time LAN Times Magazine test editing, seven books, and over a dozen certification tests as a consultant), my wife and children still recognize me as their husband and father, respectively. My portion of this book is dedicated to their steadfast support of my pursuits. Thank you Kristy, Caitlin, and Brittany.

Contents at a Glance

Table of Contents

6 IP Addressing and Configuration 73

Part III: Building and Maintaining the Server 85

7 Installing Server Applications 87

8 Maintaining the Internet Server

Part IV: System Administration   117

9 Security and Configuration   119

10 Planning for the Internet Server   137

New Riders Publishing

The staff of New Riders Publishing is committed to bringing you the very best in computer reference material. Each New Riders book is the result of months of work by authors and staff who research and refine the information contained within its covers.

As part of this commitment to you, the NRP reader, New Riders invites your input. Please let us know if you enjoy this book, if you have trouble with the information and examples presented, or if you have a suggestion for the next edition.

Please note, though: New Riders staff cannot serve as a technical resource for the Internet or Windows NT, or for related questions about software- or hardware-related problems. Please refer to the documentation that accompanies these products or to the applications' Help systems.

If you have a question or comment about any New Riders book, there are several ways to contact New Riders Publishing. We will respond to as many readers as we can. Your name, address, or phone number will never become part of a mailing list or be used for any purpose other than to help us continue to bring you the best books possible. You can write us at the following address:

New Riders Publishing
Attn: Associate Publisher
201 W. 103rd Street
Indianapolis, IN 46290

If you prefer, you can fax New Riders Publishing at (317) 581-4670.

You can send electronic mail to New Riders at the following Internet address:

Jfairweather@newriders.mcp.com

NRP is an imprint of Macmillan Computer Publishing. To obtain a catalog or information, or to purchase any Macmillan Computer Publishing book, call (800)428-5331.

Thank you for selecting *Building a Windows NT Internet Server*!

1

Introduction to the Internet

With a galaxy of tools available for communicating—from telephones and answering machines to relatively recent innovations such as voice mail, FAX machines, and satellite repositories—why would anyone suggest yet another medium?

The question is no longer simply how to store information or how to communicate one-on-one. The question is much more complex because the solution no longer deals solely with basic storage or communication. You must now take into consideration that frequently data needs to be distributed to multiple selected locations or persons in a variety of time zones.

Learning Internet Basics

As robust personal computers and high-speed communications devices dropped in price, computer users discovered the benefits of bulletin board systems (BBSes). For those of you who are not familiar with the bulletin board system concept, a BBS is a computer that is accessible typically through a telephone line and modem, and enables its users to communicate with one another electronically as well as store and retrieve various data and programs. BBSes enable you to leave electronic mail for select users, or enter online conversations with groups of people. You can upload and download files, or research topics of interest. Initial BBSes had one limitation: they were stand-alone systems, incapable of communicating with other systems.

In its most basic form, the Internet is essentially a collective set of servers located around the world, hosted by individuals, corporations, universities, and service providers. These servers are connected and act as one big bulletin board system, making information once reserved for government use available to the public. Because your initial login point through your selected Internet service provider is typically still local to your home or business, you can tap into the Internet globe for the price of a local call and a service provider fee. Thus, the information to which you have access is almost endless, and the access to it is almost instantaneous.

But what can the Internet—which is basically a collection of computer bulletin board systems—do that those tools already in place cannot? What could possibly set this network apart from other forms of communication?

No one is suggesting that the Internet should replace the communications channels currently in place. Rather, this relatively new technology should serve as a new and additional medium, one that solves unique problems others cannot.

Comparing Traditional Mediums of Communication

To put the Internet into perspective, consider other forms of communication. The telephone is still the leader for people separated by vast distances. It is ideal for sharing information that is not too complex or too lengthy. When accuracy, however, is the focus of communication—for the sharing of business facts, computer data, technical references, and so on—the phone is a poor substitute for the written word (or raw data). Writing—a letter, a report, a formally published manuscript—is the traditional medium when accuracy is essential. Writing, of course, cannot solve all communications problems. The written word, for example, cannot transfer spreadsheet data in a form that can be immediately loaded into a computer and used, even if the written text is faxed.

Further consider what might happen if the data has to be available to a number of different people scattered around the state or across the country. Switching to the telephone once again might help; a conference call could potentially be a solution. But conference calls not only take time to plan, they also require that everyone be available at exactly the same time—not always an easy trick in business. The Internet is more than ready to fill this gap between the phone call and the traditional written word.

Although you might belong to a couple of BBSes and your company has its own electronic mail system, you are still limited to the number of people and resources that you can access or with whom you can communicate. The Internet enables you to "reach out" and make use of tools throughout the world for the price of what is usually a local telephone call.

And don't limit yourself to thinking that the Internet is only of use to those who want to chat with others electronically or to those who have extensive research project requirements. For the most part, you are only limited by your imagination as to what you can accomplish with the Internet. An example of an imaginative adaptation of the Internet is that of being able to place long-distance calls using a local Internet connection. You simply use a microphone that packetizes your conversation into files and then transmits them to the receiving end to be expanded back into speech. Granted, your conversation will be broken and lag at points, but you could literally talk for hours to people around the globe for the price of a local phone call.

History of the Internet

The Internet took its first breath as a direct result of research and development requirements by the government, universities, and large corporations. As time passed and as the Internet grew, non-researchers gained access. Since that time, the Internet has grown to over 20,000 networks, bringing together almost 50 million people. For the first

time, the ceiling for the Internet's four-octet addressing scheme is in jeopardy of being maxed out.

Realize that the Internet's main purpose is to bring a multitiude of computers together in as efficient a manner as is possible to share data. It's easy to see how the apparently simple task of one computer either getting or giving data from or to another computer can get quite complex. If you only had to connect two computers, one bit would suffice (one computer would be addressed as 0, the other as 1). Double the number of computers to four and you require two bits of addressing (00, 01, 10, and 11). Double it again and you need three bits. Keep in mind that for every doubling of the number of computers (or hosts) requires the addition of another bit, a hypothetical ceiling of four sets of eight bits or 4,294,967,296 (256^4) addresses was established (with some restrictions). Specifically, class A has 2^{24} addresses (16,777,216), class B has 2^{16} addresses (65,536), and class C has 2^8 addresses (256).

The standard protocol for the Internet is Transmission Control Protocol/Internet Protocol (TCP/IP). The Defense Advanced Research Project Agency (DARPA) developed TCP/IP in 1960 to test an experimental packet-switching network. This network—ARPAnet—was meant to allow a vendor independent network that had the capabilities to grow and morph as the needs changed.

What began as an experiment became so popular that in the mid-1970's, the ARPAnet was removed from experimental status and was made available to the public. By the mid-1980s, the TCP/IP protocol suite was adopted into Military Standards (MILSTD). At that point, everyone connected to the

Internet was required to convert to these standardized protocols. This standardization was no small task, so DARPA contracted Bolt, Beranek, and Newman to put TCP/IP into what is frequently referred to as Berkeley, or BSD, Unix. This connection marked the first official set combining of TCP/IP and Unix, a protocol suite and an operating system frequently associated with one another.

Unix and TCP/IP, considered a match made in heaven, enabled a large number of computers to connect; thus the birth of the Internet—a combination of the unclassified Defense Data Network, called MILNET, and the ARPAnet. Although ARPAnet was phased out in the late-1980s to early-1990s, the Internet continues to grow at an ever-increasing rate.

ARPAnet had been funded by the government from its inception until this year. Although many Industry Analysts speculate that this lack of governmental funding will degrade much of the Internet support, an equal number of analysts believe that the Internet has become a child that has grown up and will only benefit from being "kicked out of the house."

The Internet Explosion

Try to get past the cover of any computer-related magazine without seeing something relating to the Internet. What was once restricted to Unix-based universities and government agencies is now available for Macintoshes, even DOS-based workstations. As of this writing, nearly 30 million people are using the Internet (which is comprised of over 1.5 million computers, 30,000 networks, and 200 countries). The amount of data available for a service provider fee and a local call is staggering, but the manner in which it can be accessed varies greatly (SLIP, PPP, dial-up, ISDN, "switched 56," and so forth).

Many computer-literate people still believe that the Internet is exclusively a playground for the Department of Defense (DoD) and Unix programmers. For those of you who fall into this category of believers —although until recently you might have been correct—times have changed. The Internet does indeed now offer something for nearly everyone who has a need or an interest in almost any category.

Reasons for Internet Growth

The Internet has increased in popularity for the following four reasons:

→ The people who need information are geographically dispersed, and cannot easily come together at the same time to communicate.

→ The information itself is complex, technical, lengthy, or subject to frequent changes (such as fluctuating prices or feature sets); it is all these things when accuracy is important.

→ Time is an important factor, either in the value of the information or the availability of the people who need to share it.

→ The shared information needs to be *massaged* (meaning, a word-processing document or spreadsheet data needs to be loaded into a computer on the receiving end for further processing).

Internet Connectivity Benefits

One of the main advantages the Internet has provided the typical BBS user is the ability to access data and converse with users around the globe with one local telephone call. In the past, if you wanted to retrieve data from multiple sites (or BBSes), you would have had to connect to each separately, a time-consuming and very costly task if the desired BBS were in another town, city, or country. The Internet provides a much more economical way of accessing multiple sites that are geographically distant from one another, simply because all the sites are linked together to form one very large worldwide network.

Until recently, the Internet was strictly a Unix-based system, only accessible through text-based Unix commands. You would log in to your local system, attach to other servers on the Net, and basically nose your way around the globe. This type of access was fine for the typical Unix command-line professional as the Internet was still a command-line system running the Unix operating system. But even though many computer-literate individuals find the Unix command line daunting to say the least, the resources located on the Internet were too vast to be ignored by those who knew of its existence.

Accessing the Internet

For those aware of what the Internet had to offer corporations and individuals alike, the Internet presented itself as a freeway awaiting the creation of on-ramps. People had cars (computers), and the Internet was already linking hundreds of cities (universities, corporations, and agencies). People needed some way to get on the freeway.

If only people had some form of transit system to get them from point to point; then they wouldn't need to know how to drive (that is, they wouldn't need to know how to use Unix commands). Until a short time ago there were no buses (simplified Internet-access software packages) available to the public. Either you knew Unix or you didn't travel the Internet.

Marketing personnel did, indeed, recognize the benefits of enabling public access to the freeway. But this recognition marks where the approach to the freeway ends. Although some people have requirements that stress electronic mail and passing files, others need to perform research and find data that is pertinent to their specific tasks. As users' needs vary with regard to Internet accessibility, they also vary with regard to what they look for in a car. Taking this scenario one more step, the more features you car has, the more expensive it becomes.

Reasons to Establish an Internet Presence

The reasons for establishing a presence on the Internet are only limited by the system administrator's creativity. The most obvious reason is to make accessible some form of data that would be more costly to communicate by other means. The following are a few reasons for wanting to make your presence known on the Internet.

→ Interactive Internet marketing

→ Communicating with customers instantly, including sending requested information on demand to customers using e-mail

→ Collaborating with colleagues by exchanging e-mail and files

→ Promoting your business by posting information to widely distributed Internet forums

→ Publishing information such as brochures, newsletters, and catalogs online

→ Creating virtual storefronts to generate sales directly from the Internet

→ Distributing files in any format quickly and conveniently to anyone or a select group

→ Accessing the vast resources available on the Internet, such as people, information and program files, online databases, libraries, and so on

→ Decreasing Internet accessibility

Using Windows NT as an Internet Server Platform

A plethora of reasons exists for choosing Windows NT as your Internet server platform. Security, ease of configuration, and scalability offer just a few. Just because the folks who conceived the Internet were all familiar with Unix, C programming, and sleepless nights doesn't mean that any of us have to adopt the same hobbies. Microsoft has done much to simplify Internet server management as well as to bring—until now—hidden traps to graphical light.

NT Internet Server Security

Without getting into the nuances of NT Internet server security (which is covered in Chapter 9,

"Security and Configuration"), the Windows NT product can take on various topologies to thwart potential security breaches. The most popular configurations follow:

→ Very high security using physical isolation between the Internet and your local area network

→ High security that uses protocol isolation to keep a protocol such as IPX, on your local area network side, from being accessed by the Internet IP side

→ High security using a third-party router between your local area network and the Internet access point

→ Good security levels attained by disabling TCP/IP at the NT server

→ Low security offset by putting up few restrictions and enabling TCP/IP at your NT server

Combine these topology security measures with NT's NTFS and you can tailor your NT Internet presence to be as secure as you want.

Ease of Configuration

Until NT entered the Internet server market, your options for creating an Internet server were drastically limited. The most popular option involved taking a couple years off your life to learn how to install and manage a Unix-based operating system, and then attempting your Internet presence. The second most popular solution was to select from a few different third-party software packages that sat on top of some operating system, and use that package as your Internet server package.

Benefits of Built-In Services

Microsoft Windows NT has drastically simplified the task of creating and maintaining an Internet presence. First, all the software you need to become a server is included. No hidden programs need to be purchased later; NT offers a fully featured set of Internet programs that will have you up and published in no time.

Ease of Installation and Use

Even if you are an ardent Unix professional, you probably have had to learn how to use Microsoft Windows at one time or another. The Windows platform and suite of associated programs has skyrocketed in popularity; and as easy as the basic Microsoft Windows program is to install, the Windows NT Internet server services are almost as simple.

As a point of reference, if you began your computer foray with Unix command-line utilities, those were the humble beginnings of this author as well. Although Unix is still a mainstay in my hearty computer diet, NT has proven itself to be almost as easy to install as the base Windows 3.11 package with which most are familiar.

Problems with Third-Party Products

Using NT as your Internet server eliminates all third-party package concerns. Whenever you use a third-party package on top of an operating system, you have to question how cleanly the third-party developers have developed their product and how properly they make system calls. Most people know that aside from the published program call hooks, system calls are unpublished. These calls can be changed at the discretion of the operating system developer, and only the developing engineers are the wiser. You can see the problem. If a third-party developer has used an unpublished call for any portion of his program code and the OS developer changes the call, no one knows what the outcome will be! Stay with operating systems (OS)/network operating system (NOS)-based solutions when possible.

Scalability

Many operating systems, as well as network operating systems, today require the equivalent of general anesthesia to change any of the components or peripherals. Microsoft has gone to great lengths to simplify the manner by which you modify your OS/NOS to meet the needs of you and your users. Similarly, when you use your NT server as an Internet server, you need to consider those who hook on to your machine as individual users as well.

It is easy to view your local clients as your only concern. When you think of your external Internet connection as superfluous and the users as non-users, however, you lose track of the fact that they require resources in the same manner that your local users do. Depending on the system you set up, you might run out of hard drive space and require more memory as more demands are placed on your system.

These realizations—many of which can be limited by restricting the type(s) of Internet access allowed to your system—are not intended to scare you. Rather, they are an attempt to bring to light the fact that the inherent scalability of NT makes changing your system configuration quite simple. If you find that your communications channel is your bottleneck, upgrading your transmission medium on an NT server is a simple task. Increasing RAM, upgrading a hard drive, adding an MO drive are all straightforward administrative tasks in NT. This fact only simplifies your Internet server duties.

Link Types

Windows NT supports the most common Internet service connection types. Regardless of your personal or corporate Internet-access needs, you need to take special care when selecting the Internet connection type for you. Each interface/protocol type has its own set of advantages and disadvantages, but the ultimate decision is usually cost based. With the exception of availability of certain access types (for example, ISDN), typically, the faster the pipe the higher the cost (bet that little revelation didn't catch you off-guard). The connection types supported by Windows NT include (but are not limited to) the following:

➜ PPP dial-in

➜ SLIP dial-in

➜ Dedicated PPP/SLIP

➜ 56K (a.k.a. Switched 56)

➜ PPP ISDN

➜ T1T3

Chapter 2, "Components for Connecting to the Internet," covers each of these service types in greater detail.

Summary

Whether you need only a periodic presence for a select few friends or employees to exchange data, or if you want as many strangers as possible to view a video about your corporation, the Internet can meet your needs.

Windows NT provides an efficient, cost-effective, and easy-to-maintain alternative for building an Internet server as compared to some of the other methods currently available. This book is meant to take you through the steps of implementing NT as an Internet server, and to make you aware of hardware and software options available.

Even if you are familiar with the Internet from a user standpoint, the time and effort necessary to place an Internet server into the Internet server pool is very rewarding. Depending on the type of system you want to put in place, the benefits are grand. If your goal is to offer a chat arena for people with similar likes, you will have company. If you want to offer service or support for some product, you will have customers. If you simply want to offer a place for people to come and camp, you will be deluged. "If you build it, they will come."

2

Components for
Connecting to the Internet

You have been instructed to connect your company

to the Internet, and you are trying to plan out the

resources you will need. One would assume this

to be a fairly easy task simply because of the

many Internet connectivity packages that are

available today, such as Internet-in-a-Box, Internet

in 5 Minutes, and Quick Internet Access. These

types of Internet connectivity packages, however,

are generally for the single user who needs or

wants an Internet connection.

Internet access for a network is typically much more complex than a single-user Internet connection because of the multiplicity of available options. For a network, an Internet connection is independent of the network's topology. Whether you have an Ethernet LAN, a Token Ring LAN, or an FDDI LAN, you can connect to the Internet. Connecting to the Internet, however, may have a different meaning for a LAN than for a single user—what are these differences? This book will help answer this and many other questions, including the following:

→ What does Internet connectivity entail in terms of hardware, software, and services?

→ How is Internet connectivity brought to all LAN users with the least systems management?

→ What are the different types of Internet applications available, and how do you decide to use one application over another?

→ How much bandwidth and type of wide area networking service do you need for your LANs?

→ Which service provider should you use for your Internet access?

→ How do you build a business case for Internet connectivity?

What This Book Will Do for You

The objective of *Building a Windows NT Internet Server* is to help LAN Managers, System Administrators, and MIS Managers understand all the components needed to connect their company LANs to the Internet.

The intent of this book is not to provide hands-on Internet usage exercises, but rather to bring out information that can help Network managers make the right choice of hardware, software, services, and applications.

Who Should Read This Book

This book will benefit anyone chartered with providing Internet connectivity for LANs. Specifically, people having the following job titles will benefit the most:

→ Network Managers

→ LAN Administrators

→ MIS Managers

→ Network Planners

→ Systems Engineers

→ Anyone Interested in Building a Windows NT Internet Server

End-to-End Internet Connectivity

To achieve end-to-end Internet connectivity, you must first be aware of what the Internet can do for you and your company. Chapter 3, "The Internet: Yesterday, Today, and Tomorrow," begins with a historical overview of the Internet and follows its development through today, showing how companies are maximizing their usage of the Internet for

Figure 2.1

*Internet connectivity
components.*

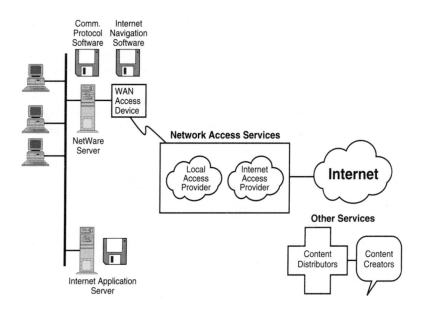

business purposes. Emerging uses of the Internet are also discussed, followed by a detailed cost and benefit analysis on how you can justify your Internet connection.

True end-to-end Internet connectivity requires additional software, hardware, and services at both the sender's and the receiver's end. Some of the existing software and hardware used for Unix computer access may be usable for Internet access, while new software and hardware may have to be acquired for transparent Internet access for all LAN users.

Figure 2.1 shows all of the components needed to connect a network to the Internet. Similarly, a mirror image of this figure would represent the other end of the Internet connection.

The Internet connectivity matrix, shown in figure 2.2, is another representation of the Internet connectivity components depicted in figure 2.1. Because this book is organized around this matrix, the remainder of this chapter focuses on each level of the matrix to lay the groundwork for future chapters.

```
 _____
(                                    )
(  Layer 7   SECURITY AND MANAGEMENT )
 )_____(
|  Layer 6  | Internet Access Providers          |
|           | (Regional, National, International) |
|-----------|------------------------------------|
|  Layer 5  | WAN Access Devices                 |
|           | (Routers, Modems, DSU/CSU)         |
|-----------|------------------------------------|
|  Layer 4  | WAN Access Services                |
|           | (Analog, ISDN, Leased, Switched 56, Frame Relay) |
|-----------|------------------------------------|
|  Layer 3  | Internet Application Servers       |
|           | (E-mail servers, News servers, Web servers) |
|-----------|------------------------------------|
|  Layer 2  | Internet Navigation Software       |
|           | (E-mail, FTP, Telnet, Mosaic)      |
|-----------|------------------------------------|
|  Layer 1  | Network Communication Protocols    |
|           | (IP, IPX, AppleTalk)               |
```

Figure 2.2

The Internet connectivity matrix.

Network Communication Protocols

The communication protocol understood by the Internet is *Internet Protocol* (IP). To help you understand IP and IPX, Chapter 5, "Understanding TCP/IP," provides an overview of the IP protocol; and Chapter 6, "IP Addressing and Configuration," discusses the issues related to administration of the Windows NT TCP/IP environment.

Internet Navigation Software

The Internet is like a country without road signs. People who have been traveling on the Internet for some time know of many back alleys and shortcuts, but those less familiar with it tend to get lost.

These old-timers also tend to use archaic navigational aids, which are command-line-oriented applications. Many people, however, are now contributing to the development of much-needed maps to make it easy for everyone to navigate the Internet. Many new tools have thus been developed to facilitate Internet navigation, with Mosaic perhaps being the most well-known tool. Similarly, FTP and Telnet tools are becoming more graphical and easier to use. Other navigational aids such as Archie, WAIS, and Gopher are making it easier to find resources on the Internet. These tools are collectively called *Internet applications*. Appendix B, "Guide to Client Applications," discusses the various Internet applications that are needed by end users to navigate the Internet.

Internet Application Servers

How are your users going to get their e-mail? Where is the e-mail going to be stored? In what format do your users use e-mail today? How can your Lotus cc:Mail users send and receive mail from the Internet? The answers to these and similar questions might indicate the need for an e-mail server. Where should that server be located—at your site or the Internet access provider's site? The same questions need to be answered for News servers or Web servers. Chapter 7, "Installing Server Applications," provides the answers to these questions by examining issues involving the various Internet servers and offering different alternatives for diverse situations.

WAN Access Services

The next level on the Internet connectivity matrix is selection of the WAN services. In most cases, you can find an Internet Access Provider within your local telephone calling area. Therefore, you need to be concerned only with WAN service from your local telephone company. How much bandwidth is required by the LAN users? What is your monthly budget for access services? What kind of bandwidth pattern do you expect on your WAN? If your bandwidth requirement is 56 Kbps, what types of services are available, and how do you decide between each of the services? Chapter 4, "Internet Access Services," addresses these and many other similar issues, and provides an overview of different WAN services, such as analog dial-up, digital dial-up, and dedicated lines.

WAN Access Devices

Specific hardware devices are needed to connect a network to the appropriate WAN access service. This WAN device might be just a modem, a router with a modem, an ISDN terminal adapter, or a leased line DSU/CSU. Chapter 4 covers some of these details relating to WAN access devices, and defines which options are appropriate for different situations.

Internet Access Providers

In order to access the Internet, you need to have an *Internet Access Provider* (IAP). It is similar in concept to the long-distance service provider needed for your telephone service. Appendix A, "Internet Service Providers," provides a list of the IAPs.

Security and Management

Internet security is a key issue that should be a proactive part of planning the Internet connection, rather than a reactive part or merely an afterthought. Security issues should not be restricted to just controlling access from the outside, but they also should focus on controlling access from the inside to provide management information and details of Internet connectivity. Chapter 9, "Security and Configuration," discusses the issue of security and management tools for Windows NT-centric LANs.

Benefits of LAN-Based versus Single-User Internet Access

Do you let your LAN users attach a modem to each individual PC for remote access? Do you let your LAN users connect to other LANs over modems attached directly to their computers? Do you let your LAN users have a FAX modem in each of their own computers? Most likely, you probably answered "No" in each case. The most common reasons for this are as follows:

→ Reduced costs by sharing the telephone lines

→ Reduced costs by sharing modems and other hardware

→ More controlled and secure access

→ Easier to manage and administer

 Do you know how many users on your LAN already have a dial-up Internet access account? It is time to think of providing Internet access to all LAN users before dial-up single-user access gets out of hand.

These same reasons can be applied to the issues surrounding Internet access that affect your network users. Unfortunately, many companies today are letting users connect directly to the Internet with a modem on their desktop. This method can be both inefficient and expensive if the goal is to give all employees Internet access. It is best to consider providing Internet access to all of the users on your LAN with usage permission restrictions in place, which provides more management leverage and control. More importantly, however, is that appropriate bandwidth can be allocated, depending on the total concurrent usage. Therefore, with the benefits of a LAN-based Internet connection in mind, go now to Chapter 3, where you will continue to learn more about the components for connecting Windows NT to the Internet.

3

The Internet: Yesterday, Today, and Tomorrow

It is very difficult to define the Internet—it means different things to different people. For some people, it is an online service that offers entertainment and educational value. For others, it is just another wide area network that provides an economical means for both inter- and intra-company electronic communications. The Internet has also been called an online library of software and ideas, as well as published materials such as books and magazines. Technically, the Internet is the largest *Transmission Control Protocol/Internet Protocol* (TCP/IP) internetwork in the world.

The following all describe the concept of the Internet from different perspectives:

→ Internet = Inter + Net = Connection of different nets = The Net

→ Collection of computers linked together in one large network

→ World's largest bulletin board

→ World's largest electronic mail network

→ World's largest online service

The Internetworking Concept

It is much easier to understand the concept of the Internet by comparing it to an internetwork. An *internetwork* is a group of network nodes communicating over the same or different physical medium (such as twisted-pair wiring or fiber wiring) or topologies (such as Ethernet or Token Ring) that are linked together with a bridge or a router. *Bridges* or *routers* can be thought of as traffic cops in the sense that they direct the data from one network to another. The internetworking of LANs that are geographically separate is done using a *wide area network* (WAN) service, such as a dedicated service (T-1, Frame Relay, or 56/64 Kbps links) or a switched connection (Dial-up Analog, ISDN, or Switched 56). Once an internetwork is in place, users are able to access resources on any of the other LANs, provided those users have the appropriate access privileges.

Figure 3.1 shows an internetwork of a company with three geographically separate LANs connected together to form a large virtual LAN. These LANs are connected over a dedicated wide area network.

The Internet—the Internetwork of Networks

The Internet is a large internetwork comprised of many LANs and computers. Unlike the internetwork of a company that only connects its own offices together, the Internet connects networks and computers from any number of organizations. These networks and computers can be located anywhere in the world. If you have access to the Internet, therefore, you can connect to another host computer on the Internet that may be located next door to you or in a foreign country thousands of miles away. This, of course, all occurs behind the scenes and is transparent to the user.

As shown in figure 3.2, the Internet is very similar in concept to the internetwork of a company like that shown in figure 3.1. The only difference is that the Internet is larger than any single internetwork, is open to anyone, and may cross many more LANs to get to the destination.

It is estimated that over 3 million hosts are connected to the Internet, and these hosts are located in more than 50 countries. The number of users now using the Internet is estimated to be anywhere from 10 million to 35 million.

 n o t e As defined by the InterNIC, an Internet *host* is a computer or a collection of computers directly connected to the Internet, which enables network users temporary access to its services. The computer acts as "host" to one or more public services and the users accessing those services.

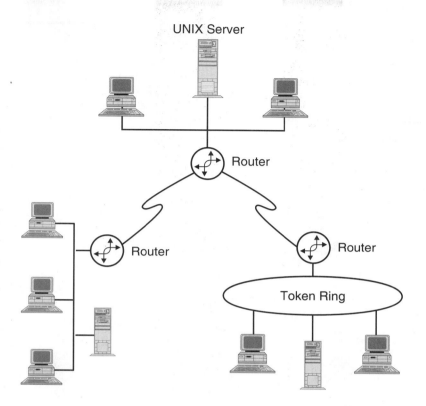

UNIX Server

Router

Router

Router

Token Ring

Figure 3.1

Internetworking makes all LANs appear as one.

One might expect such a large internetwork to be controlled and managed by many network managers. Despite being the largest internetwork in the world, the Internet is virtually anarchic and runs without any centralized authority or management, with the exception of the InterNIC. In order to understand how this large and very public internetwork functions efficiently without any central management, let us first look at a brief history of the Internet.

 n o t e The *Internet Network Information Center* (InterNIC), or simply *The NIC*, is an organization that provides information and registration services to Internet users. One of the primary responsibilities of the InterNIC is assigning IP addresses and domain names to new Internet sites and keeping track of these Internet addresses to avoid duplication. The NIC is also responsible for maintaining and distributing *Requests for Comments* (RFCs)—technical reports that document protocols, standards, and policies on the Internet.

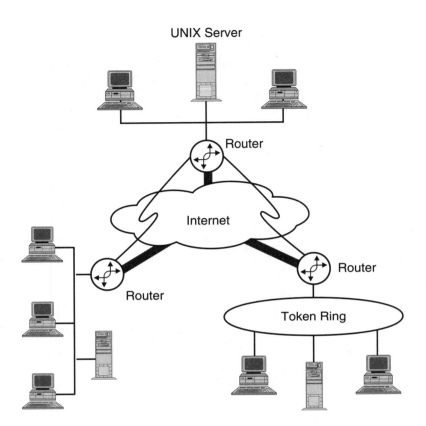

UNIX Server

Router

Internet

Router

Router

Token Ring

Figure 3.2

The Internet is an internetwork of computers worldwide.

History of the Internet

The Internet was called ARPAnet at the time of its origination in 1969. The *Advanced Research Project Agency* (ARPA) is an agency of the U.S. Department of Defense that contracted with *Bolt, Beranek, and Newman* (BBN) to set up a WAN to connect four university sites for research purposes—Stanford, UCLA, UC Santa Barbara, and the University of Utah. The *Internet Protocol* (IP) was born out of the ARPAnet project. In the early 1980s, the Department of Defense separated out MILNET, the military portion of the ARPAnet, and left the remainder of the ARPAnet for use by the Universities.

The *National Science Foundation* (NSF), another agency of the U.S. government, laid the foundation for the modern-day Internet when it decided to build its own network to connect six supercomputer centers. NSF used ARPAnet's IP to build its network, which was connected using 56 *Kilobits per second* (Kbps) links. The usage of the NSFnet started increasing as many local schools connected to their nearest supercomputing center for access to the Net. In 1987, NSF awarded a contract to Merit Networks Inc., which ran Michigan's educational network in partnership with IBM and MCI. This contract was meant to upgrade the network to a high-speed (T1-1.544 *Megabits per second* or Mbps) backbone. As the traffic increased, NSF upgraded its backbone to T3 (45 Mbps) speeds in 1992. NSFnet completely phased out ARPAnet in the early '90s as the U.S. Department of Defense started using MILNET for classified purposes, while all other traffic from ARPAnet migrated to the NSFnet.

 The six supercomputing centers linked initially by NSF were as follows:

→ Cornell National Supercomputer Facility, Cornell University

→ The Scientific Computing Division of the National Center for Atmospheric Research, Boulder, Colorado

→ San Diego Supercomputer Center, University of California

→ National Center for Supercomputing Applications, University of Illinois

→ John von Neumann National Supercomputer Center, Princeton, New Jersey

→ Pittsburgh Supercomputer Center, operated jointly by Westinghouse Electric Corp., Carnegie Mellon University and the University of Pittsburgh

Use of the NSFnet for commercial purposes initially created a huge controversy because it was originally founded for research purposes only. Now that the U.S. government's funding of the NSFnet has expired, however, both commercial and noncommercial traffic can be carried freely and without dispute on the NSFnet, now known as the Internet.

Internet Access Providers

All Internet subscribers pay for the Internet in the form of monthly fees to their particular *Internet Access Provider* (IAP). The IAPs buy their communication circuits from telephone companies and also buy access to a Network Access Point where they can connect to the Internet. A Network Access Point is a tap into the Internet backbone that provides worldwide connectivity. Alternatively, IAPs can pay a yearly fee to *Commercial Internet Exchange* (CIX) for carrying commercial traffic among providers. The CIX charges every Internet access provider an annual fee of approximately $10,000.

 CIX was formed by three IAPs—CERFnet, PSInet, and Alternet—with an objective to provide commercial high-speed networking services without using the NSFnet. It is not a requirement for an IAP to be a CIX member.

The Internet Access Provider industry began as a cottage industry, with many Internet operators working out of their living rooms using just a few Unix workstations and modems. Because Internet access is now becoming mission-critical for many companies, however, IAPs are being asked to provide a much greater level of service to their customers than ever before. The Internet industry therefore is evolving, resulting in fewer but larger IAPs that are better equipped to provide more reliable service. Many of the telephone companies, such as Sprint, AT&T, and MCI, are now providing Internet access, making it a very competitive market. In addition, all of the online service providers, such as CompuServe, Prodigy, and America Online (AOL), are starting to offer direct Internet services. All of these changes will make the Internet very different from what it is today.

Development of Internet Standards

The Internet Society (ISOC) is a nonprofit voluntary member organization that promotes the Internet and its technologies. The Internet Society appoints a council of invited volunteers, which forms what is known as the Internet Architecture Board (IAB). IAB's charter is to deal with standardization and long-term directions for the Internet.

The Internet provides its users with an opportunity to express their opinions and get involved through the Internet Engineering Task Force (IETF). The IETF is a voluntary organization—anyone can attend its meetings. The IETF has published many standards to help the networking industry develop interoperable products. The IETF sets up working groups to address specific issues. Generally, when there are at least eight volunteers from different companies to research a topic, a working group is formed. In the end, most working groups publish a document known as Request for Comments (RFC), which becomes a standard. Over one thousand RFCs are available on many different topics, including SNMP, TCP, IP, UDP, PPP, and many more. These RFCs can be obtained from the InterNIC by way of U.S. postal mail, electronic mail, or with an Internet file transfer program.

The Internet Today

The number of hosts on the Internet has been growing at an estimated rate of 10–20 percent per month from early 1993 to 1995. Figures indicate that the number of Internet hosts exceeded 3 million at the end of 1994, as shown in figure 3.3. Assuming an

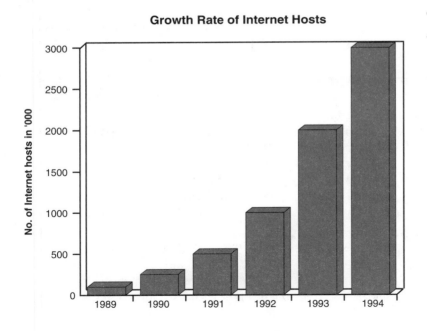

Growth Rate of Internet Hosts

Figure 3.3

The growth rate of Internet hosts.

average of 10 users per host, this points to over 30 million possible users. Another Internet growth indicator is the increased amount of traffic, which is measured in gigabytes on a monthly basis by the Internet Society. Figure 3.4 displays a graphical representation of Internet traffic patterns.

Even though the United States accounts for over 50 percent of Internet hosts, European and Asian hosts are also growing at a rapid rate, as shown in figure 3.5. As stated previously in this chapter, over 50 countries have host computers on the Internet. Universities are often the first to get connected to the Internet in these countries. Developing countries, however, face great obstacles to such growth. As an example, one of the primary obstacles to Internet growth in developing countries is the lack of reliable telephone service. If this were not an issue, you would see a much greater growth rate in the number of Internet hosts worldwide than what you have seen thus far.

Figure 3.4

Traffic growth on the Internet.

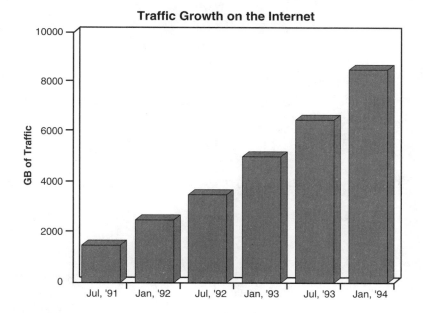

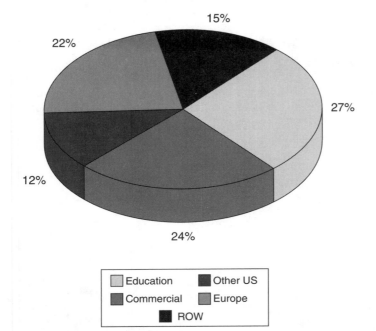

Current Internet Hosts Distribution

15%

22%

27%

12%

24%

Education Other US
Commercial Europe
ROW

Business Uses of the Internet

The Internet is used in the corporate environment in a variety of ways. The following discussion relates some of the most important uses to date, including electronic mail, research, and technical support.

Electronic Mail

The most common application for which people are using the Internet is e-mail. The only universal standard for exchanging e-mail among heterogeneous mail systems is the Internet mail standard, called

simple mail transfer protocol (SMTP). Even when you send an e-mail message from CompuServe to a user on a different online service, such as America Online, you still use the Internet to exchange e-mail. The following example depicts this usage well.

It is 9:00 a.m. in New York, and you want to make sure that your vendor in California gets your message as soon as he arrives at the office. You could wait and call him when it is 9:00 a.m. in California, but you have a lunch meeting at that time. Another option would be to leave him a voice mail message, but the details of your message are too complicated. Thus, the best solution is to leave him an electronic mail message with all the details. Despite the fact that your vendor uses a different electronic mail system and is not directly connected to your LAN, you can still communicate with one another by using the Internet and/or Internet mail protocol.

Just as FAX numbers on business cards are considered a necessity today, an Internet e-mail address will be a must within the next 12–18 months. Most companies in the high-technology business already include an Internet e-mail address on their employees' business cards.

Research

The amount of material available on the Internet well exceeds that of many libraries, and a common complaint has been simply the difficulty in finding that information. However, this problem is resolving itself with the newer Internet tools that are becoming available. One of the most important tools in this category is a program called Mosaic, which allows a point-and-click search of Internet information. These types of tools definitely provide an advantage to the user and make the job of finding information on the Internet much easier. Again, an example of this Internet usage method follows.

You have been assigned the task of evaluating different routers for your company, and you have a week to complete the project. You recall several articles in a recent trade magazine, but you can't locate the magazine. Because you have an Internet connection, however, you can view all previous issues of the magazine online, find the articles for which you are searching, and print the ones you need. To get a copy of one of the vendor's product brochures, you can get back on the Internet and browse for the information from the vendor's Web

server. Now, in just a matter of hours, you have all the basic information to get started with your evaluation.

Electronic Technical Support

Many companies, including Cisco, Microsoft, and Novell, are using the Internet as a technical support vehicle for customers. In essence, customers can use the Internet in lieu of making a telephone call to get marketing information, software updates, and other types of technical support from an organization. This type of usage is very similar to the services provided by vendor bulletin boards and CompuServe forums, with the major differences being economics and accessibility. Internet access is more universal than CompuServe, and it is in many situations much cheaper to set up a company's bulletin board on the Internet than on CompuServe. Using the Internet for technical support enables companies to provide services that they could not otherwise offer.

The various ways in which technical support is being provided by companies include the following:

➜ **E-mail.** Using e-mail, phone tag can be avoided, offering customers a timely response to their requests.

➜ **FTP.** FTP access means that a company can offer both the textual and binary files for downloading by its customers. For example, Microsoft offers bug fixes for their software via FTP.

➜ **Web servers.** Web servers are primarily being used to provide information rich with text, graphics, and multimedia. Unlike FTP access, where one file is loaded at a time and then viewed at customer site, Web servers enable customers to view the document before making a decision on whether they should download that information.

Emerging Uses of the Internet

One of the emerging uses of the Internet is electronic telemarketing, which provides an alternative to traditional telemarketing. As shown in figure 3.6, traditional telemarketing is very expensive, especially for a small company—the result is either losing customer calls or employing more staff than needed. Also, traditional telemarketing uses the same skill-level person to answer technical questions as it does to take down a name and send literature.

As it enters the electronic age, a company provides all its literature and other pricing-related information on a Web server, which provides customers with the chance to browse and download the desired information instead of making a telephone call to get answers to specific questions. Therefore, electronic telemarketing complements traditional telemarketing, reducing the cost of doing business (see fig. 3.7). Electronic telemarketing will enable smaller companies to offer as high quality of service as any large company.

Another emerging use of the Internet is that it is becoming a de facto WAN for small and mid-size companies that cannot afford to have their own private network. In this case, small companies receive the same benefit of interconnectivity that large companies have enjoyed for years. For the Internet to become such a de facto WAN, however, issues such as security and privacy need to be addressed. These issues will be covered in more detail in Chapter 9, "Security and Configuration."

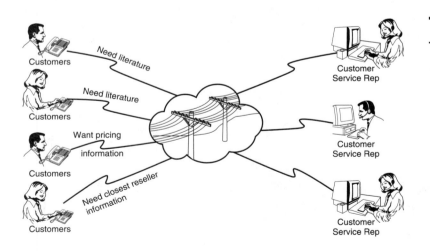

Figure 3.6

Traditional telemarketing.

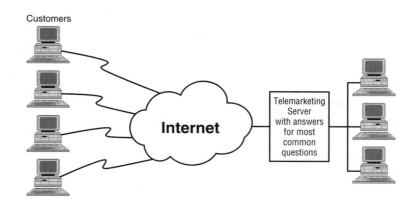

Figure 3.7

Traditional telemarketing, as supplemented by electronic telemarketing.

Electronic commerce will begin to evolve as standards for digital cash and secure transactions are accepted by developers and users of the Internet. Some rudimentary form of electronic commerce is already emerging on the Internet, where products can be ordered over the Internet once the account information has been verified using the traditional methods of a person-to-person call.

Lastly, some other emerging uses of the Internet appear in the area of video conferencing techniques, as well as multimedia commercials and product advertising on the Internet. Companies with Web sites are already starting to implement intensive graphics on their home page to make their site more appealing to the public, as well as to better sell their products to customers.

Justifying Internet Connectivity in Your Corporation

With the emerging uses of the Internet essentially upon us, there is a mad rush in the corporate world to establish Internet presence—this means different things to different people, however. For some companies, getting a company domain name is the highest priority; for others, it is using a public e-mail system; and for others, establishing their own Web server on the Internet is a priority.

The first task is to analyze the needs for the Internet connection by considering the following questions:

➜ What will the Internet do for me?

➜ Why should I connect to the Internet?

Second, the benefits from the Internet connection must be evaluated. The benefits achieved will vary from company to company, but can essentially be clarified by asking the following questions:

➜ What tangible benefits can be gained by connecting to the Internet? The primary measurement here is financial. In this section, the cost benefits obtained from the Internet connection is discussed.

➜ What intangible benefits can be gained by the Internet connection? While these are often the most difficult benefits to measure, they may in fact be the determining factors that justify the Internet connection. A number of these intangible benefits are discussed later in this chapter.

Third, the cost for the Internet connection must be considered. There are many options to be factored into this portion of the analysis. Many Internet Access Providers have varying service offerings and costs. In addition, many options are available for connecting to the Internet. The connection may be via analog dial-up using a modem connected to a standard telephone line, circuit or digital switched services such as ISDN or Switched 56 Kbps, point-to-point dedicated circuits such as a T1 circuit, or packet switched services such as Frame Relay. In Chapter 4, "Internet Access Services," a detailed presentation of each technology, its benefits, and respective costs will be discussed in detail.

Finally, these three areas must be considered in whole to determine if the Internet connection is feasible. It is unlikely that the tangible cost benefits of the Internet connection will equal or exceed the costs involved. However, by evaluating the needs and the overall benefits of connecting to the Internet, you, like many organizations throughout the world, may determine that the Internet community is one of which you need to be a member.

In the remainder of this chapter, a presentation of the justification of the Internet connection is provided, with emphasis in the following areas:

➡ Cost savings

➡ Improved customer service

➡ Information access

Cost Savings

Cost savings are typically the first argument in favor of an Internet connection. Before the cost savings can be measured, however, you must assess how exactly the connection is to be used.

Using the Internet for Electronic Mail

One of the most common uses for the Internet connection is electronic mail. Assessing the cost savings of an Internet connection by taking advantage of electronic mail is very straightforward. To assess this benefit, you must first estimate the costs and characteristics of traditional means of communication, including mail via the United States Postal System, overnight mailing via providers such as Federal Express and United Parcel Service, and voice communications—particularly long distance communications.

 It must be emphasized that electronic mail should not be considered as a replacement for all written and verbal communications within an organization and externally to customers, vendors, or business partners. Electronic mail should be used where appropriate and not considered as a replacement for traditional means of direct, personal communication.

For example, one organization provided the following information, which was gathered through interviews with departmental representatives and analyzing expenses related to postage, overnight letter shipments, and long distance phone calls. Each department was asked to monitor what percentage of their mailings, overnight mailings, and telephone costs could be made effectively and appropriately by way of electronic mail. Over a ninety-day period, the following average expenses, representing the amounts which could potentially be saved with electronic mail, were demonstrated:

Mail postage	$325
Letters via overnight services	$140
Paper savings (stationery, envelopes, and so on)	$78
Long distance telephone expenses	$225

Using this organization as an example, an Internet connection could provide for a tangible cost reduction in these expense categories in excess of $750.

However, there are also intangible cost advantages in using electronic mail, particularly when compared to the U.S. postal mail system. Electronic mail is delivered virtually immediately, whereas traditional mail may require several days to even a week to be delivered. Will your customer benefit by receiving your information that same day, while your competitor's information may not arrive for a week? Will your sales representative in a remote sales office benefit from receiving new pricing information immediately without having to wait several days? Will informing your employees of new procedures and policies reduce costly mistakes in manufacturing? Frequently, the intangible benefits will provide savings that may even exceed those that can be directly measured.

Using the Internet as a Wide Area Network

Perhaps the second most used feature of the Internet is its use as a *wide area network* (WAN)

for a corporation with geographically dispersed locations. Many organizations may choose to build a private WAN using services and circuits provided by one of many WAN service providers. The primary benefit of this approach is security—the private WAN is isolated from other WANs. The issue of security is discussed in detail in Chapter 9, "Security and Configuration." Yet while this isolation provides strong security benefits, it may also be its greatest limitation. A private WAN will not facilitate communications with people outside of the company WAN, such as customers, vendors, and business partners.

Using the Internet as a WAN will facilitate communication with other organizations and individuals that are connected to the Internet. Furthermore, the Internet connection may in fact present cost savings when compared to building a private wide area network.

Improved Customer Service

In today's ever-competitive business environment, customer service and customer satisfaction are often considered as critical to an organization's success as the financial indicators. In the eyes of many companies, customer satisfaction and financial success often go hand in hand. But how can the Internet be used to improve customer service?

Consider the example of a company whose primary business is the manufacturing and sales of computer networking equipment. Traditionally, technical support for this type of company is accomplished by staffing a help desk or technical support center with technically qualified personnel to assist in answering questions and resolving problems for its customers. The cost of this approach is fairly easy to assess. Tracking personnel costs and related expenses such as telephone services can be tracked very accurately, and can also be readily used in the financial justification of an Internet connection. Using the Internet as a means to provide customer assistance and support, an organization can realize savings by controlling telephone expenses, as well as functioning with less staff than otherwise required.

A customer would contact this support center with the expectation of prompt and accurate information. If this information can be provided to the customer electronically via the Internet, information and solutions can be provided immediately. Chapter 7, "Installing Server Applications," presents a number of Internet access methods, including Telnet access, Web servers using HTTP, and file transfer using FTP. For example, access to a database application providing technical information, tips, and product information could be provided to customers using Telnet. This same information could also be provided using a highly graphical interface using *HyperText Transfer Protocol* (HTTP) by providing access from Web browsers, such as NCSA Mosaic or Netscape. Required files, such as software updates and bug fixes, could be transferred using FTP.

But what are the benefits? First, the obvious benefit would be a tangible financial benefit to the company. Customers that use these online services to obtain their information would not require the involvement of an individual from the technical support and the related costs with traditional forms of support, such as telephone expenses.

Finally, let's review the effectiveness of the preceding example. The organization discussed previously indicated that the applications that have been developed for Internet access are utilized on average 1,300 times per week, while the average contact when using traditional telephone support is 12 minutes. This would provide for an elimination of more than 100 person-hours in support costs per week. Additionally, whereas software might have been provided to the customer via overnight mail, the customer can now download the required files through the Internet, eliminating overnight mailing charges. Clearly, this is a considerable savings.

But even more important is the benefit to the customer. Accessing an application via Telnet or HTTP in real time enables a customer to obtain information immediately. This information could be accessible 24 hours per day, even when support personnel are not available. Customers can receive the resolution they require promptly without the time constraints of when the support center is open or when a representative is available to assist them. The organization discussed previously has realized a 20 percent increase in customer satisfaction survey results in the first year alone.

Information Access

One of the most rapidly growing uses of the Internet is for the sales and marketing of products and services. As more individuals and organizations connect to the Internet, the Internet becomes an increasingly viable and productive medium for communications.

Perhaps one of most significant driving factors for this growth is the expanding use of Web servers and browsers. Through the use of a Web server, these applications enable a company to provide information to its customer in a highly graphical format that is easy to use.

Many companies in the computer system and networking market, such as Apple Computers, Cisco Systems, Hewlett Packard, IBM, Microsoft, Novell, Sun Microsystems, 3COM, and many others, are currently using Web servers to communicate information to their customer and prospects. Technical associations such as the InterNIC, the Internet Engineering Task Force (IETF), the Internet Society, and the ATM forum are using Web servers to make their information available to a large audience. Many computer magazines today are being presented electronically via Web servers. Demographic data, financial market indicators, corporate financial information, and endless other topics are being presented on the Internet using Web servers. It should be no surprise that the Internet is sometimes referred to as the "library of the future."

A Web browser enables the user not only to access these graphically based servers, but also to search the Internet for sources of information. Using the online directories and various search tools, you can search the Internet for information on any number of topics.

There are benefits to this growth both for the organization providing the information, as well as to those who access it. Using this technology enables a company to make its marketing literature, product announcements, and public pricing available to a large audience without the costs associated with printing and distributing written information. Changes to this information can be made immediately without the costs and delays involved with printed materials.

The benefit to the user is the immediate accessibility of information. There is a vast amount of information on the Internet, and the tools available today make this information very accessible.

Evaluating the Issues

The first step to justifying an Internet connection is performing a needs analysis, which should include the factors that are demanding the services that will be made available from the Internet, the type of connection to the Internet that will be required, and the equipment that will be required. By measuring the benefits that will be derived from the Internet connection, the feasibility of connecting to the Internet can then be properly evaluated.

Summary

The Internet is over 25 years old, but its commercialization and thereby explosive growth has occurred only in the last few years. E-mail continues to be the number-one application for the Internet. Using the Internet for research is getting easier with a new class of point-and-click Internet navigational tools, such as Mosaic. The Internet is being used by many companies for providing better service to their customers at a cost lower than the traditional methods. Justifying an Internet connection is best accomplished by first performing a needs analysis, and then by measuring the costs and benefits that will result from connecting and not connecting to the Internet. It is likely that when you compile all of the tangible and intangible benefits, they will outweigh the costs of an Internet connection in today's ever competitive business environment.

p a r t
•••

Hardware and Software Requirements

4

Internet Access Services

Most network managers say that they can never have enough bandwidth, especially when it comes to wide area networking (WAN). Unlike LAN bandwidth, however, WAN bandwidth is not free. Generally, bandwidth price is directly proportional to its size—a 384 Kbps link costs more than a 56 Kbps link, for example. The monthly cost of WAN services is a significant portion of the total monthly cost of Internet access. Selecting the right amount of bandwidth and the right type of WAN access service is critical. Realistically assess your bandwidth needs, evaluate different services in relation to your needs, and then select an Internet Access Provider (IAP) that offers the best type and WAN bandwidth service.

This chapter provides guidelines for determining the optimum WAN service for your needs, including bandwidth calculations and types of service. The following WAN services are discussed:

→ Analog dial-up services

→ Switched digital services, including ISDN and Switched 56

→ Dedicated WAN services, including Frame Relay and Point-to-Point Leased (or Dedicated) lines

In addition to discussing different services, information is also provided on the types of devices needed at the customer premises to take advantage of different WAN services.

 n o t e This chapter focuses on layer 4 of the Internet connectivity matrix.

7 SECURITY AND MANAGEMENT
6 Internet Access Providers
5 WAN Access Devices
4 WAN Access Services
3 Internet Application Servers
2 Internet Navigation Software
1 Network Communication Protocols

Understanding WAN Services

Before delving into a discussion of the different WAN services, it is essential to understand how WAN services function. Traditional data and voice networks connecting any two offices within the U.S. use a local and a long-distance provider. The local access provider connects your premises to their nearest central office, where the call is then handed off to the long distance access provider. The same process is mirrored at the sender's end, where the long distance provider hands off the call to the local access provider. The geographic location of the hand-off points on the long-distance network is referred to as *Point of Presence* (POP). Sometimes the same telephone company is both the local and long-distance provider. Figure 4.1 illustrates a typical scenario for traditional WAN services.

Local access in the U.S. is generally provided by the seven *regional bell operating companies* (RBOCs)—Ameritech, Bell Atlantic, Bell South, NYNEX, Pacific Bell, Southwestern Bell, and US West. In addition, many smaller local access providers exist. Telephone companies such as AT&T, MCI, and Sprint provide long-distance access for WAN services. In most of the European and Asian countries, local and long-distance access is provided by one centralized telephone company. There is a recent trend in many European countries (such as the U.K.), however, toward decentralized and multiple telephone carrier systems.

As in a traditional WAN service, you need two types of WAN service providers for Internet access— local and long-distance. Internet Access Providers

Figure 4.1

*An example of typical
call routing for traditional
WAN services.*

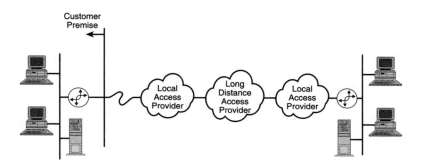

(IAPs) are in a sense the long-distance carriers for Internet access, while local access is still provided by the RBOCs. Most IAPs lease their lines from long-distance carriers, thus acting as distributors for the long-distance services. Figure 4.2 shows a typical arrangement of Internet access, with local access being provided by an RBOC going into the POP of the IAP. The IAP then in turn connects to the Internet, using telephone lines leased from the telephone companies.

Telephone companies such as MCI and Sprint have recently entered the Internet access business, while many of the other telephone companies, such as AT&T and the RBOCs, have also announced their intentions to enter the business. Some online services like CompuServe have their own private networks, giving you the choice of using just their network or using their network as an access point to the Internet. Only a few IAPs have their own private network.

Figure 4.2

*A typical arrangement of
Internet access.*

Types of WAN Services

There is no universal way to categorize services offered by telephone companies. For the purpose of this book, WAN services are categorized into the following two areas:

→ Dial-up or switched WAN services

→ Dedicated WAN services

Dial-Up Services versus Dedicated Services

As the name indicates, dial-up services are not always "on," whereas dedicated services are up 24 hours a day whether someone is using them or not. In dial-up, you pay for what you use (the amount of time the connection is up)—the connection times are metered. With dedicated connections, however, you essentially "lease" the line and pay a fee that is independent of the usage level. Your dial-up service can be used in a dedicated line mode, however, if the connection is kept open all the time to a pre-set location. This is very common for Internet access in cases where only a local "unmetered" call is needed from your house or office to the nearest IAP.

From an IAP's standpoint, if the IAP does not have to assign a static IP address and dedicate a port and a modem specifically for the customer, it is a dial-up service. The IAP will not wake up your host for a dial-up connection—in other words, it won't call your computer if someone on the Internet wants to access your host when you are not connected to the Internet. In figure 4.3, for example, if User X wants to FTP or Telnet into Host A on a LAN that is connected to the Internet using a dial-up service, the user won't be able to complete the connection unless someone from the LAN first dials a connection to the Internet.

When an IAP assigns a static IP address, and dedicates a port and a modem specifically to a customer, it becomes a virtual dedicated link. The type of WAN service can be either a permanent connection or a dial-up connection that is kept on all the time. Most IAPs that provide dedicated analog service (as discussed in the following sections) recommend leaving the dial-up link connected all the time to make it a virtually dedicated link.

Figure 4.4 shows an example of a dial-up service, which appears as a dedicated link to users dialing in from the Internet because the connection is kept on all the time. When User X requests a connection to Host A, the IAP dials into Host A's LAN. The delay caused by setting up the dialed connection is small. From User X's perspective, Host A has a permanent connection to the Internet.

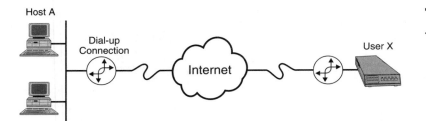

Host A

Dial-up Connection

Internet

User X

Figure 4.3

The outside user can't initiate a call into the dial-up account.

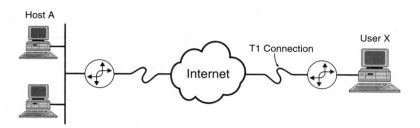

Figure 4.4

A dial-up connection can appear as a permanent connection to outside users.

A dial-up service from an IAP's standpoint thus may not always be the same as it is from a WAN access provider's point of view. In the past, all dial-up services were predominately analog, while most of the dedicated link services were digital. That distinction is no longer valid due to new advances in dial-up technology. The next section provides details on different dial-up WAN services from the standpoint of the WAN access provider.

Dial-Up WAN Services

Dial-up WAN services, which enable you to connect any two points in the world, do not provide a permanent connection. The connection is made on an as-needed basis, and you pay only for the time duration of the connection. A device such as a telephone or a modem is required to initiate the connection. Dial-up WAN services can be further categorized into universally available analog dial-up services and dial-up digital or switched digital services, which include ISDN (most popular), Switched 56 Kbps, and others. The discussion that follows first focuses on analog dial-up services, and then progresses into switched digital services.

Analog transmissions follow voice patterns and have voltage levels that vary continuously. Digital transmissions translate all data into 1s and 0s. All

of the computer-generated data that is digital in form is thus converted into analog signal (using modems) before being sent on the telephone wire. The physical telephone wiring for both analog and digital dial-up is the same—it is a copper wire pair that runs into the majority of houses within the U.S. The difference in the analog and digital dial-up, however, comes from the central office switch to which the lines are connected.

Analog Dial-Up Services

Analog dial-up service—also called *Plain Old Telephone Service* (POTS)—is the only service that is available worldwide. Most homes in the U.S. and the rest of the world receive this type of service from their telephone companies. Analog dial-up delivers the most economical service, but it offers the least amount of bandwidth. In most places, selecting an IAP that has a POP in the local calling area is economical—analog dial-up services are not metered within a local calling distance.

Accessing Analog Dial-Up Services

Analog dial-up service can be obtained either directly from your local telephone company or by putting an analog line card in a *private branch exchange* (PBX). All data applications, as opposed to voice applications, require a modem. The modem converts the digital data generated by computers into analog signals for sending it over the telephone wire. The maximum theoretical bandwidth from an analog line is 32 Kbps. With the recent advance in modem technology, today's modems can provide 28 Kbps of raw throughput.

Modem Standards

You know that your old modem was rated for 57.6 Kbps, but the maximum theoretically possible bandwidth is only 32 Kbps. How is that possible? Both are correct statements, but the statements refer to different data rates. The following list explains the modem terms that are important to understand before you can make an intelligent modem selection:

→ **Raw throughput.** This is the maximum throughput in *bits per second* (bps) that you can expect from your modem with no compression. Depending on the line conditions and the modem at the other end, you may make a connection at this speed or drop down to the next fallback speed. A modem with raw throughput of 14.4 Kbps may not be able to connect with another modem at 14.4 Kbps, for example, and therefore may only make an actual connection at 9600 bps, due to either line conditions or the receiving modem. Some of the standards such as V.32, V.32bis, and V.34, set by CCITT, specify the maximum throughput.

→ **Error correction.** V.42 and MNP4 are the most common standards; most modems come with the V.42 error correction protocol. The error correction protocols were developed to counter some of the errors introduced by line quality and distortion. MNP10 is another standard used in cellular systems for error correction.

→ **Compression.** Most modems today use the V.42bis as the default compression standard. Under the ideal condition for compression (generally a blank file), V.42bis will yield a 4:1 compression, which is how a 14.4 Kbps modem was marketed as 57.6 Kbps modem; the reality, however, is a compression rate of 2:1. V.42bis only provides compression for text files, and not for binary files. Most binary files available for download on the Internet are compressed with PKZIP or some other compression scheme.

→ **Fallback.** Before the V.34 standard came into existence, most modems dropped to the next lower speed standard if they could not make a connection at their rated speed. With the V.34 standard, modems fall back in decrements of less than 100 bps. Because V.34 is still a new standard, the same vendor's modem should be used at both ends of the connection to get the full performance benefit.

Table 4.1 provides a list of the most commonly available modems and their specifications.

 n o t e Contrary to popular opinion, you can have your own domain name even if you have a dial-up account. You can have domain name of mycompany.com, for example, even if you have an analog dial-up service.

Choosing Analog Dial-Up for Your Internet Connection

For a single user Internet connection, many people choose the analog dial-up service because it provides an easy platform for connecting to the Internet. For a LAN connection to the Internet, the decision to select analog dial-up services depends on your current and estimated future usage of the Internet.

The following criteria can be used to help determine if analog dial-up is the appropriate choice for your LAN-based Internet connection:

→ Do you need both inbound and outbound Internet access? If you need only outbound Internet access, analog dial-up is sufficient. Outbound access enables users on your LAN to access the Internet, but customers could not access your servers unless you initiate the connection to the Internet. Inbound access permits outside users to access your Internet servers that are made available for their use, thus making your Web server available for your customers to access product information. For inbound access to servers like FTP, Gopher, and Web, analog dial-up is insufficient.

→ How many users on your network have access to the Internet? The general rule of thumb is that analog dial-up access may suffice for a network of up to five users.

→ What are the most common applications used? Each application has a different Internet bandwidth requirement. If the application does not require a large bandwidth, an analog dial-up service is usually an acceptable option.

→ On most networks, e-mail is the number one Internet application. If e-mail is your only Internet application, analog dial-up service is sufficient for large numbers of users; however, if you need to receive your e-mail instantly, analog dial-up service is inadequate because you have to dial your IAP's host to check mail. Also, dial-up service is inadequate if your users send files frequently with their e-mail.

→ FTP access is generally not very bandwidth-intensive except when a file is being transferred. In average settings, not many people are transferring files with FTP simultaneously, so an analog service should be adequate.

→ Web access requires more bandwidth than any other Internet applications. Even for a

Table 4.1 Modem Specifications

Modem Modulation Standard	Maximum or Advertised Throughput	Raw Throughput	Average	Fallback Throughput
V.32	38.4 Kbps	9600 bps	19.2 Kbps	4800 bps, 2400 bps
V.32bis	57.6 Kbps	14.4 Kbps	28.8 Kbps	12, 9.6, 7.2 Kbps
V.34	115.2 Kbps	28.8 Kbps	57.6 Kbps	<100 bps increments

 * Advertised throughput is 4 times the raw throughput and assumes that the modem has V.42bis compression
** Average throughput is generally twice that of the raw throughput

single user, analog access at V.34 speeds is inadequate. If your users want Web access, analog dial-up access is not recommended for LANs.

→ What about my budget? There are two types of monthly charges—one for the local telephone access into the nearest location of the IAP, and one for the services provided by the IAP, such as access into the Internet. Analog access is the cheapest of all WAN access services, costing between $25 and $100 for unlimited usage depending on your local phone company's tariff structure. Most IAPs charge anywhere from $20 to $150 for unlimited analog access.

In some states, like California, ISDN access is very competitive with analog access. Therefore, you must compare access prices before making a decision.

Switched Digital Services

Switched digital (or dial-up digital) services have become popular in the last few years. The most commonly available switched digital service in the U.S. is Switched 56 Kbps. ISDN, however, is quickly becoming the universal standard for switched digital access in today's environment. ISDN is now readily available in most metropolitan areas within the U.S. and in most industrial countries such as Japan, Germany, U.K., and France.

Integrated Services Digital Network

Integrated Services Digital Network (ISDN) is a set of digital transmission protocols defined by CCITT, the international standards organization for telephony and telegraphy. The protocols are accepted as standard by virtually all the world's

telecommunications carriers. ISDN provides end-to-end digital connectivity. Unlike dial-up analog service, data travels in digital form all the way from the sender's computer or telephone, to the central office of the telephone company, to the long distance provider, to the central office, and then to the computer or telephone of the receiver. Unlike dial-up analog services, ISDN also offers the ability to carry both data and voice simultaneously over the same connection. In addition to providing an integrated voice and data service on a digital network (hence its name), ISDN also offers higher bandwidth than dial-up analog services.

There are different types of ISDN services, with *Basic Rate Interface* (BRI) being the most common. The other type of ISDN is called *Primary Rate Interface* (PRI), which is equivalent to T1 services. PRI is discussed later in this chapter. BRI consists of two 64 Kbps B channels and one 16 Kbps D channel (see fig. 4.5). The two B channels carry the actual customer data; whereas, the D channel carries the signaling information that is needed by the telephone company. The D channel is therefore a separate out-of-band signaling channel for ISDN services.

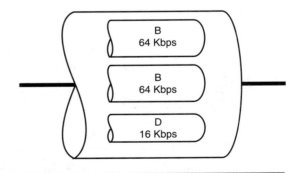

Figure 4.5

BRI is comprised of two B channels and one D channel.

note ISDN can be thought of as a collection of independent channels—you can reserve specific channels for certain applications, or you can combine channels together for higher throughput.

In the first case, one of the B channels is used for voice, and the other B channel is used for data application, such as Internet access. In the second case, both B channels are used for data, but are going to different locations within the network. Two B channels can also be connected to the same location, with each B channel's bandwidth combined for data applications to generate a higher throughput.

The process of combining two B channels to give a higher resultant throughput is called *inverse multiplexing*. In an ideal situation, inverse multiplexing of two B channels will result in a bandwidth of 128 Kbps (64 *2). The telephone system within North America has not been completely upgraded to accommodate ISDN signaling. Therefore, you may not get more than 56 Kbps from each B channel or 112 Kbps from the two B channels.

One of the other benefits of ISDN, besides the higher throughput, is having a very fast call set-up. Analog call set-up takes as long as 30 seconds; whereas, the call set-up on ISDN is less than five seconds. Users with their LANs connected to the Internet with ISDN will thus be able to make the connection much more quickly than users connected with analog dial-up lines.

Also, the pricing of ISDN ranges from $25–$100 depending on the region. In some areas, the price directly correlates with the amount of usage, whereas other areas simply charge a flat rate. Table 4.2 lists the typical pricing structures available through the telephone companies.

Table 4.2

ISDN Pricing Structure

Carrier	Monthly Rate	Usage Charges
Ameritech	$34.15	Voice and data: 1–16 cents per minute (depending on time of day)
Bell Atlantic	$23.00	Voice: 2.9 cents per minute Data: 5 cents per minute
BellSouth Telecommunications	$99.50	Circuit-switched voice and Data: no charge Packet-switched data: 0.000214 to 0.000257 cents per minute
GTE Telephone Operations	$69.37	Voice: no charge Data: 3–5 cents first minute; 2–3 cents each additional

continues

Carrier	Monthly Rate	Usage Charges
Nynex	$28.23	Voice: 8 cents first minute; 1.3 cents each additional Data: 9 cents first minute; 2.3 cents each additional
Pacific Bell	$26.85	Voice and data: 4 cents first minute; 1 cent each additional
Southwestern Bell Telecommunications	$46.00	No usage charges

Table 4.2, Continued

ISDN Pricing Structure

Depending on the tariff structure and your usage, ISDN may turn out to be cheaper than Point-to-Point Dedicated lines for the same bandwidth. For areas where there are no usage charges, an ISDN line can be left connected all the time, thus getting a virtual leased line connection for the price of ISDN. Generally, the installation charges for ISDN are also less than the Point-to-Point Dedicated lines.

Accessing ISDN Services

ISDN service, like analog dial-up service, can be ordered either directly from your local telephone company or by putting an ISDN line card in a *private branch exchange* (PBX). ISDN utilizes the same pair of copper wiring that is used by analog dial-up lines. Therefore, if you wanted to get an ISDN service at home, no additional wiring will be needed in most cases. ISDN is now available in all major metropolitan areas—Bell Atlantic, Pacific Bell, and Ameritech are leaders in providing ISDN access within their respective service areas.

Connecting ISDN to Your Network

Just as connecting to the Internet using analog services requires a modem, ISDN requires a terminal adapter. The terminal adapter connects the computer with the telephone company network. Figure 4.6 shows how to connect your network to the ISDN network. The terminal adapter doesn't connect directly into the telephone jack. A network termination unit (NT1) is needed, in addition to the terminal adapter. The NT1 device provides the power for the network, as well as the proper signaling protocol. More and more terminal adapter vendors are incorporating the NT1 into the terminal adapter. With an integrated NT1/terminal adapter, you can connect directly to your telephone jack. Most of the time, it is preferable to have an integrated NT1 because it is one less external device to manage.

Because terminal adapters are all different, it is important to understand your requirements. If you are getting ISDN specifically for an Internet connection, you will need a terminal adapter that supports two data channels and the capability to inverse multiplex the two channels for a higher throughput. The standard on the Internet for inverse multiplexing is called *multilink point-to-point control* (an extension of the PPP protocol). Currently,

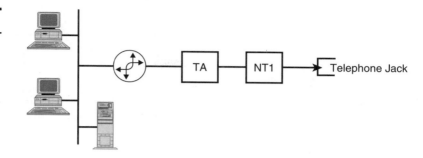

Figure 4.6

BRI ISDN connections require a terminal adapter and NT1 device.

no products conform to that standard. This situation is likely to change very quickly; at this time, however, most of the terminal adapters have their own proprietary method of inverse multiplexing, which means you must use the same terminal adapter on both ends of the ISDN connection. This is why many IAPs insist you use a particular brand of terminal adapter for ISDN service.

The raw throughput you can expect from a BRI connection is 64 Kbps or 128 Kbps. You would expect that you could increase the throughput with some compression scheme, as is the case with modems. Unfortunately, there is no standard compression scheme for ISDN terminal adapters yet; however, an effort is under way to come up with a compression standard. You will start to see standard-based compression in all the ISDN terminal adapters in the near future. As is the case with inverse multiplexing, standards for compression don't exist, leading to incompatibilities between different terminal adapters. For now, keep in mind that the equipment at your end must be compatible with the equipment at the service provider's end.

Switched 56 Kbps

Switched 56 Kbps is another switched data service that is similar to ISDN. In the same manner as ISDN,

you can call up bandwidth when needed. Unlike ISDN, however, Switched 56 Kbps is a single channel service that can only carry data. Switched 56 Kbps is only available in the North American circuits—no equivalent exists in Europe and Asia. Switched 56 Kbps, unlike ISDN, has no separate signaling channel, has only in-band signaling, but is available in most places. When you compare it to either ISDN or to analog services, it is relatively expensive. Switched 56 Kbps probably won't be a very desirable service beyond the next few years because of the advent of ISDN and *Frame Relay*, a packet switched service discussed later in this chapter.

In order to connect to a Switched 56 Kbps service, you need a *data service unit/channel service unit* (DSU/CSU). A DSU/CSU connects any external Switched 56 Kbps connection to your network. The DSU part of the system converts data into the correct format, and the CSU part of the system terminates the line condition, conditions the signal, and participates in the testing of the connection.

Choosing a Switched Digital Service for Your Internet Connection

For a LAN connection to the Internet, the decision to select a switched digital service depends on your current and estimated future usage of the Internet. The same criteria discussed previously under "Choosing Analog Dial-Up for Your Internet Connection" can also be used to help determine if a switched digital service is the appropriate choice for your LAN-based Internet connection.

Outbound Internet Access?

For outbound access, switched digital services offer two benefits over analog connections—faster call setup time and more bandwidth. For inbound access, ISDN can be used in place of Point-to-Point Dedicated lines if it is economical to leave the line connected all the time.

Internet Usage

The following rule of thumb may help you estimate your company's Internet usage amount. ISDN access with two B channels inverse multiplexed is sufficient for between 25–50 users; whereas, for 25 users or less, ISDN single B or Switched 56 Kbps is appropriate.

Internet Application Usage

What are the most common applications used? Each of the applications, along with its usage pattern, require a different bandwidth. Some applications, such as e-mail and Telnet, take up less bandwidth, while applications such as Web access require large bandwidth.

E-mail and FTP Bandwidth Requirements

E-mail does not require much bandwidth because it is a store-and-forward system. Users do not expect mail they send to arrive instantly, and their computer is not tied up while the mail is making its way through the Internet to its recipient. ISDN or analog access are both appropriate for traditional e-mail users, but as users begin using more MIME-based e-mail (which tends to have many file attachments, such as Microsoft Word document or Lotus spreadsheets), the e-mail application will require a high bandwidth connection such as ISDN.

File transfer with FTP will benefit by higher bandwidth provided by ISDN. If your users download many files from the Internet, they will save significant time with an ISDN connection.

Web Access

The application that benefits the most from an ISDN connection is the World Wide Web. Most Web browsers are not optimized for slower speed modems, so any amount of high bandwidth provided to a Web application will make a noticeable difference. The increase in ISDN bandwidth by four times over the analog connection delivers dramatic improvements when it comes to Web access.

 n o t e The following is a guideline for calculating bandwidth requirements for a LAN:

→ **E-mail (ASCII-based).** 2 Kbps/user.

→ **E-mail (MIME-based).** 5 Kbps/user.

→ **Web access.** 10 Kbps/user.

For a five-user LAN with two active e-mail users and three active Web users, you thus need a bandwidth of 50 Kbps for optimum access.

Budget

In some parts of the country, such as the area served by Pacific Bell, a small monthly price difference exists between analog access and ISDN access. ISDN gives you substantially more bandwidth than analog—therefore, choosing between the two is an easy decision. Most of the IAPs charge more for ISDN access than for analog access, however. Some IAPs offer a fixed price ISDN service, where the IAP actually pays for the cost of the ISDN access and usage. These access and usage charges are budgeted, however, into the fixed price that is actually offered, so it may or may not be a less expensive option.

If you are accessing the Internet 4–6 hours per day or more, a Point-to-Point Dedicated line or Frame Relay (both discussed later in this chapter) may be more economical than using switched digital services. Carefully consider your usage pattern before choosing ISDN or Switched 56 Kbps.

Dedicated WAN Services

Dedicated services are the second most used services after analog access because they are available everywhere and can be configured for different speeds. The most common speed for dedicated lines is 56 Kbps in the U.S., and 64 Kbps in Europe and Asia. Dedicated services can be further categorized into Packet Switched services and Point-to- Point Dedicated services.

Packet Switched Services—Frame Relay

One of the newest technologies to emerge in the last few years in the area of wide area networking

is called Frame Relay. Frame Relay is a packet switching protocol with speed ranges from 56 Kbps to 45 Mbps. Frame Relay delivers a low delay, high throughput connection. Frame Relay is similar to the X.25 protocol, but it does not correct errors or request retransmission. Instead, Frame Relay relies on availability of superior quality lines, such as fiber, that are common in today's telephone networks. Frame Relay expects clear, high-quality lines to guarantee virtually error-free transmissions. If errors do occur, it is the responsibility of intelligent end devices to request retransmission.

Frame Relay is yet another wide area service that provides high-speed connections. Frame Relay is more of a substitute for dedicated connections rather than for an analog dial-up or switched digital connection. One of the big benefits Frame Relay offers is that the price is distance-insensitive—the distance the call travels does not affect the hourly rate for the call. That is why Frame Relay is being used extensively in the wide area networking environments of different companies. If Frame Relay is already a standard for your wide area communications, use it to connect to the Internet. Frame Relay standards already guarantee interpretability with the Internet protocol, and are set by the Frame Relay Forum.

Frame Relay is a lower layer service—there are implementations available for both IPX and IP over Frame Relay. In the OSI model hierarchy shown in figure 4.7, Frame Relay is at the data link layer. If you are using Frame Relay to connect to the Internet, you need to run IP over your Frame Relay connection. Standard RFC 1274 exists to ensure the interoperability of different vendors' implementation of IP over Frame Relay, which is suitable for all the bursty applications. Because the traffic on the Internet is not constant but goes up and down, Internet access can be classified as a bursty application.

Frame Relay	OSI Model
	Application
	Presentation
	Session
TCP or SPX	Transport
IP or IPX	Network
Frame Relay	Data Link
Physical	Physical

Frame Relay   **OSI Model**

Figure 4.7

Frame Relay protocols versus the OSI model.

Permanent Virtual Circuits

A Frame Relay connection is made up of one or more *permanent virtual circuits* (PVCs). A PVC is a dedicated, end-to-end, logical connection that is used for data transfer. Unlike Point-to-Point Dedicated lines, PVCs are not connection-oriented. They get set up like a dedicated line and remain active until the service is terminated, creating virtual dedicated connections as opposed to real permanent connections.

Committed Information Rate

Committed information rate (CIR) is defined as a minimum average data rate that the network guarantees to carry over a given PVC for a specified period. The data rate is chosen at the time of subscription, but it can be modified if users finds that their transmission needs have changed. CIR is important because a Frame Relay network may specify a throughput of 64 Kbps or 56 Kbps and a CIR of zero. A CIR is a guarantee that whenever you connect, your throughput will not fall below the threshold specified. In order to provide a CIR above zero, the phone company or access provider must reserve a physical line for your connection. If you purchase a PVC with 56 Kbps of throughput and a CIR of zero, you are not guaranteed any bandwidth. Today, the current state of the Frame Relay infrastructure is such that most users are able to get the full extent of the bandwidth. Frame Relay offers some interesting possibilities when it comes to looking at Internet connections.

Some IAPs, such as PSI, have their own private networks, enabling them to offer multiple PVCs into your network—one PVC is dedicated to one application while the other PVC is designated for a different application. One of the PVCs might be dedicated to news groups, for example, guaranteeing news groups bandwidth regardless of the level of user activity in other Internet applications. A PVC dedicated to outside users dialing into a network prevents the network from getting bogged down for inside users. This is one benefit Frame Relay offers over T1 leased lines or other dedicated lines. This advantage may also apply when comparing Frame Relay and switched digital services (i.e., ISDN, Switched 56 Kbps, etc.), depending on the customer usage of the Internet.

Figure 4.8 provides a visual example of the PVCs going to different locations.

Figure 4.8

Frame Relay PVCs can be set to guarantee bandwidth for different applications.

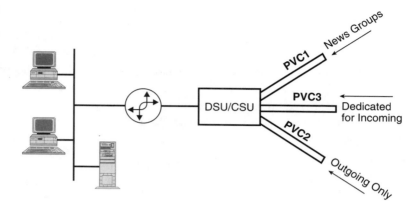

t i p   Reserving PVCs for particular applications is one way to effectively manage your Internet bandwidth.

Procuring Access Lines for the Frame Relay

Your local access provider can deliver Frame Relay, but if you already have a data multiplexer within your company and you subscribe to the Frame Relay service, use one of the PVCs to access the Internet. Most IAPs that offer a Frame Relay service assist with all the procurement of the local access services. To connect your network to the Internet using Frame Relay, a DSU/CSU is needed. In addition, you will need a router that supports routing of IP over Frame Relay protocol.

Frame Relay Pricing

Frame Relay pricing, like all other services, involves installation charges and monthly usage charges. The monthly usage charge for 56 Kbps Frame Relay is around $200 to $300. The Frame Relay pricing appears more attractive than a 56 Kbps dedicated line until you read the fine print and see that these prices are for 0 CIR. The installation charges for Frame Relay can sometimes be quite costly—as high as

$1,000. Most of the IAPs offer Frame Relay access either at the same or lower pricing than an equivalent Point-to-Point Dedicated line.

Point-to-Point Dedicated Services

Previously, the T1 trunk was the high-end option for Point-to-Point Dedicated lines, and is the one that is still most frequently used. A T1 trunk supports transfer speeds up to 1.544 megabits per second. In Europe, E1 is the equivalent service, offering bandwidth of up to 2.048 Mbps. For companies that don't require this much throughput, telephone companies have begun offering *Fractional T1* (FT1) services. FT1 services are configured as a number of 56 Kbps channels. In spite of the popularity of the T1 service, the emerging high end option for a Point-to Point-Dedicated connection is the T3 line, which supports a 45 Mbps connection. Today, very few sites in the country require a T3 line as their Internet connection, and this will most likely continue to be the case for the immediate future. Only when you start using much higher bandwidth applications, or start to use the Internet as a wide area backbone, is this likely to change.

An important difference between Point-to-Point Dedicated lines and Frame Relay is that with the latter, you are not guaranteed any bandwidth above your CIR. At first glance, Point-to-Point Dedicated line prices may look expensive for long distances (they are priced based on bandwidth and the distance between two points). Because you need the dedicated line only from your LAN to the nearest point of presence of your IAP, however, the actual cost for a dedicated line can be very reasonable. Of course, this depends on finding a suitable Internet Access Provider close to your network. Actual costs of Point-to-Point Dedicated lines range from $200–$300 within a 20-mile radius. These numbers vary between different telephone companies. Many sites connect to the Internet using Point-to-Point Dedicated lines because of the numerous benefits this type of service offers.

Accessing Point-to-Point Dedicated Services

First, check with your telecommunications manager. You may already have leased a full T1 line for voice and other services. In this case, your company may have spare channels that can be used for your Internet connection. This happens frequently when the cost of a full T1 is less than the cost of buying exactly the needed amount of FT1 services. If your company does not already have a dedicated line, contact your telephone company or Internet Access Provider.

Choosing a Dedicated Service for Your Internet Connection

Frame Relay and Point-to-Point Dedicated lines are both recommended services if you need to support both inbound and outbound Internet connections, or if you intend to host your own Web server. If you are using Frame Relay for 56 Kbps connections, your actual bandwidth will be identical to a Switched 56 Kbps or ISDN connection.

The actual throughput your applications see does not vary significantly between Frame Relay and Point-to-Point Dedicated lines. The primary economic benefit of Frame Relay—distance-insensitive pricing—is inconsequential when connecting to the Internet since most companies can find an Internet Access provider located relatively nearby. For this reason, Point-to-Point Dedicated lines are a popular alternative for companies requiring a high-speed permanent Internet connection.

Summary

Table 4.3 summarizes the types of connections you should consider for your Internet connection.

Hardware and Software Requirements

Table 4.3

Comparison of WAN Access Services

	Analog	ISDN	Switched 56 Kbps	Frame Relay	Point to Point Dedicated
Bandwidth	14.4 or 28.8 Kbps	56/64 or 112/128 Kbps	56 Kbps	56 Kbps to 1.5 Mbps	56 Kbps to 1.5 Mbps
Call Setup Time	30 seconds and up	Less than 5 seconds	Less than 20 seconds	Negligible	None
Tariff Structure	Fixed or Per Minute	Fixed or Per Minute	Fixed or Per Minute	Fixed	Fixed
Availability	High	Medium	High	Medium	High
Suitable for Inbound Access	Only if line is kept on all the time	Only if line is kept on all the time	Only if line is kept on all the time	Yes	Yes

Dial-up analog access is appropriate for single users or small LANs with up to five users. If ISDN is available in your area, its pricing may be very competitive with the dial-up analog, especially when you consider the extra bandwidth provided. For a LAN of up to 50 users, ISDN is a good alternative. For more than 50 users, or to set up your own Web servers, use either Frame Relay or a Point-to-Point Dedicated line, depending on which is cheaper in your area. Choosing the right connection up front is important because of the specialized hardware and installation charges involved.

Understanding TCP/IP

One of the first tasks you need to perform in setting up your Windows NT server for use on the Internet is to install the TCP/IP protocol. The TCP/IP protocol is the protocol all systems use to communicate on the Internet. Microsoft, recognizing the importance of this protocol, has included support in the base Windows NT system. Before you can do much of anything on the Internet, you need to install and configure this protocol. This chapter teaches you how to do just that.

This chapter covers the following topics:

→ Introduction to the TCP/IP protocol stack

→ Basic IP addressing

→ Installing Windows NT's TCP/IP support

→ Using basic TCP/IP utilities

Defining the TCP/IP Protocol

TCP/IP, which stands for Transmission Control Protocol/Internet Protocol, actually refers to a suite of protocols that facilitate the passing of data between computers on a network. It is *the* protocol of the Internet and is used to communicate on a global basis.

TCP/IP became so popular in government, education, commercial organizations, and the scientific community that it grew to be the de facto standard for internetwork communication. Because almost all modern computer systems now support TCP/IP, it is the most commonly accepted protocol available. Even small networks, made up of just a few computers, often use TCP/IP to communicate because it is so widely supported.

A Brief History of TCP/IP

The Internet grew out of an earlier network called ARPAnet. ARPAnet, which stands for the Advanced Research Projects Agency's Network, entered service in 1971. Two important requirements developed from this network: the need to transfer files

and the need to support remote logins. The first requirement later led to the development of the *file transfer protocol* (FTP), and the latter requirement led to the development of Telnet and rlogin.

It became apparent that a standard protocol would need to be developed to facilitate communication between systems. TCP/IP was proposed in 1973, but wasn't standardized until 1982. The protocol didn't become popular until 1983, when the University of California at Berkeley released a version of Unix that incorporated TCP/IP as a transport protocol. Because Unix was so widely used on ARPAnet, TCP/IP gained wide acceptance.

The IP Protocol Suite

TCP and IP are just two members of the IP protocol suite. IP is the protocol that provides the simple delivery of packets within a system. IP packets incorporate a checksum to confirm packet integrity, but apart from that, no inherent mechanisms exist to guarantee delivery. IP packets could, by themselves, get lost on the wire or arrive at their destination out of sequence.

 Checksum represents a value that is computed to help ensure that data is transmitted without error.

TCP guarantees the proper delivery of a packet to its destination. In addition, TCP also ensures that packets arrive in correct sequence. Hence, TCP provides the reliability of the communication. Its information is encapsulated within IP, and the two together form the basis of IP networking.

TCP/IP's Architecture

The designers of TCP/IP took a layered approach when they built this protocol. A layered protocol offers many benefits. Because each layer is independent of the others, changes in certain services of the protocol shouldn't affect other services. In addition, layers allow several small services to be developed for a specific task. Designing a protocol in a layered fashion is more difficult initially, but because changes and additions can be made quickly and easily, it is ultimately more efficient.

TCP/IP is not the only layered protocol. It actually follows (rather loosely) the reference model developed by the *International Organization of Standards* (ISO). The ISO, founded in 1946, drafts many standards, including information processing. It developed the *Open Systems Interconnection* (OSI) reference model for worldwide communications. The reference model defined a framework for implementing protocols in seven layers—the application, presentation, session, transport, network, data link, and physical layers.

According to the model, when information passes from computer to computer through a protocol, control of the data passes from one layer to the next starting at the application layer in one system. It then proceeds to the bottom layer of that same system, over the wire to the next system, then back up the hierarchy in that second system (see fig. 5.1). The layers are defined as follows:

→ **Layer 7—The Application Layer.** This layer is the interface point between the OSI stack and the user, and most commonly is in the form of a program or application. Common functions include opening, closing, reading, writing, and transferring files.

→ **Layer 6—The Presentation Layer.** Application programs and terminal handler programs are translated in this layer. Typically, this is done through formatting and data translation. This layer also is used for encryption and decryption.

→ **Layer 5—The Session Layer.** This layer is where communication between cooperating applications is controlled. In practice, the session layer often is not used or is incorporated into the Transport layer.

→ **Layer 4—The Transport Layer.** End-point data transferal, end-to-end data recovery, and flow control occur here. This is the layer that detects if a packet has been routed. It also ensures that all of the data has been transferred.

→ **Layer 3—The Network Layer.** Connections are established, maintained, and terminated at this layer. The network also enables the upper layers to be independent from the data transmission and switching technologies. It performs the switching functions in routable protocols, such as IP.

→ **Layer 2—The Data Link Layer.** Synchronization, error control, and flow control are maintained here to ensure that data crosses the physical layer and is reliable. The data link layer, examples of which include Ethernet, Token Ring, and FDDI, is responsible for the validity and integrity of the transmission.

→ **Layer 1—The Physical Layer.** This layer, which consists of the physical cabling of a network system (i.e., fiber, coax, twisted pair, etc.), is the physical link between the hosts.

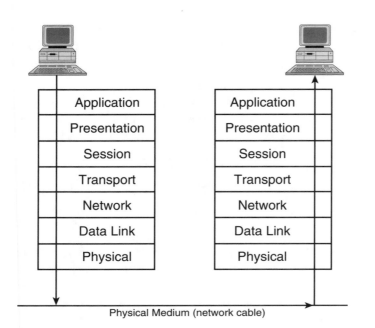

Figure 5.1

The transport of data across the OSI model.

Physical Medium (network cable)

Although no protocol follows the OSI model exactly, most of the functionality provided by each layer exists in all networks. Most systems (like IP) incorporate two or three layers into one (see fig. 5.2) because there are some protocols which can span more than one layer in the OSI model.

TCP/IP consists of only five layers, performing the functions of OSI's seven. These layers are as follows:

→**Layer 5—The Application Layer.** Applications such as FTP, Telnet, SMTP, and NFS relate to this layer.

→**Layer 4—The Transport Layer.** In this layer, TCP and UDP add transport data to the packet and pass it to the Internet layer.

OSI	TCP/IP
Application	Application
Presentation	
Session	
Transport	Transport
Network	Internet
Data Link	Network Interface
Physical	Physical

Figure 5.2

A comparison of the OSI seven-layer and the TCP/IP five-layer stacks.

→**Layer 3—The Internet Layer.** When you initiate an action on your local host (or initiating host) that is to be performed or responded to on a remote host (or receiving host), this layer takes the package from the transport layer and adds IP information before passing it on to the network interface layer.

→**Layer 2—The Network Interface Layer.** This is the network device as the host, or local computer, sees it. It is through this medium that the data is passed to the physical layer.

→**Layer 1—The Physical Layer.** Layer 1 is literally the Ethernet, Point-to-Point Protocol (PPP), or Serial Line Interface Protocol (SLIP) itself.

Each layer adds its own header and trailer data, encapsulating the message from the layer above. At the receiving host, the data is stripped, one layer at a time, and the information is passed to the next highest level until it again reaches the application host.

To facilitate network communications in Windows NT, Microsoft developed the *Transport Driver* *Interface* (TDI). The TDI provides communication between the session and transport layers of the OSI reference model. The Server and Redirector services on a Windows NT computer communicate with the transport protocols by means of the TDI (see fig. 5.3).

 Windows NT uses the Windows Sockets 1.1 interface for communication with TCP/IP applications. It is a version of the Sockets interface originally developed for Unix computers.

Other IP Protocols

Windows NT also includes User Datagram Protocol (UDP), Address Resolution Protocol (ARP), and Internet Control Message Protocol (ICMP). Each of these are part of the IP suite.

UDP is a simple protocol that an application program might use to send a packet to an application program on another machine. UDP does not guarantee delivery, nor does it guarantee that those deliveries will be kept in proper order. The

Figure 5.3

How protocols communicate with the network services on a Windows NT computer.

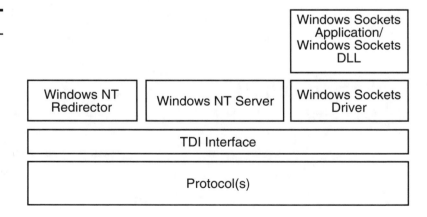

application that uses UDP, therefore, must have the built-in mechanisms for implementing retransmissions. The *Network File System* (NFS) is a distributed file system developed by Sun Microsystems that uses UDP for transport.

ARP and ICMP are maintenance protocols that support IP. They are associated with many of the utilities used on an IP network. Even though you set your own IP address when configuring your system for IP networking, for example, the protocols need to know the hardware address of each computer with which it communicates. ARP takes care of this task for you by associating the IP address with the physical address of the network adapter.

Once ARP has made the association, the data can be stored in cache. Because the ARP packets can be broadcast across the network, the replies can be read by other nodes that also can use the information. To view the ARP data, type **arp** at a command prompt on the server.

ICMP packets are encapsulated in IP packets to get node status information. The ping utility (covered later in this chapter) uses ICMP to see if another node on the network is functional. When you install IP, ping is one of the first utilities you use to see if your system is configured properly.

Understanding IP Addressing

Before an IP packet can begin its journey, it has to know where it is going. This is where IP addressing comes in. An *IP address* is comprised of a set of four cells. A period separates each cell:

132.147.160.200. The address identifies a host on the network and specifies routing information. IP addresses provide an identifier to nodes on a network so that they don't have to rely on hardware to ensure unique addressing. These cell numbers can range from 0 to 255, but some combinations are reserved for special uses.

IP addresses are separated into three classes. The first cell determines which class the address falls under. If the first cell is a number between 1 and 126, it's a class A address. If it falls between 128 and 191, it's a class B address; if it's between 192 and 223, it's a class C. Classes are used to differentiate between network sizes and types.

People use classes to accommodate networks of varying sizes (see fig. 5.4). A class A address uses the first of the four cells for a network ID and the last three for host IDs. Class A addresses are primarily reserved for networks with a large number of nodes because any combination of the last three cells can be unique to a node. A class B address uses the first two cells for a network ID; a class C uses the first three. Most small networks use class C addresses, in which only the last cell is needed as a unique node identifier.

 If you do not plan to connect to an outside network like the Internet, the class your address falls under is irrelevant. Theoretically, you can choose any network address as long as it conforms to the proper syntax. The *Internet Assigned Numbers Authority* (IANA), however, has reserved specific IP address blocks for private networks. See RFC 1597 for more details. Adhere to the guidelines proposed in this document to ensure compatibility with Internet guidelines (in the event you ever want to connect your network to the Internet).

Figure 5.4

Each address class supports a different number of networks and hosts.

Class	Address Examples				Number of nodes per network
A	100	100	100	100	16,777,216
B	150	100	100	100	65,534
C	200	100	100	100	254

If you want get your own IP address for your company rather than have a service provider assign one to you, you need to apply for and register an IP address with the Internetwork Network Information Center (InterNIC). Its address, phone number, and Internet address are as follows:

> InterNIC Registration Services
> c/o Network Solutions
> 505 Huntmar Park Drive
> Herndon, VA 22070
> (800)444–4345
> (703)742–0400
> (703)742–4811 (fax)
> hostmater@internic.net (email)

A node uses the IP address to determine which packets to receive and which to ignore. Only nodes with the same network ID accept each other's broadcasts. The node uses *netmasks* to determine which cells represent the network ID and which represent the host ID.

Netmasks

The netmask strips the network ID from the IP address, leaving only the host ID. A netmask number resembles an IP address—it contains four cells separated by periods. The only numbers it uses, however, are 255 and 0. A number 255 indicates a cell reserved for the network ID. A 0 indicates a cell reserved for the host ID.

When you assign an IP address and a netmask setting to a node, you are essentially telling it how to interpret incoming broadcasts. The default netmask setting for a class C address is 255.255.255.0. To a node, the first three cells signify the network ID; the last, therefore, is the host ID.

The most practical use of netmasking is to split your network into subnets. Perhaps you have enough nodes and networks to justify applying for a class B address, for example, and you are assigned the network ID 132.147.*xxx.xxx*. Your company, however, actually has 10 LANs with 100 nodes each. You want your networks to communicate with each other, but you don't want to apply for 10 different network IDs.

The third cell of your IP address can be used as a subnet ID. You define the netmask setting 255.255.255.0, effectively splitting your address into 256 class C networks. Each of your LANs is assigned a third cell number that they use for throughout. Each node is assigned a unique host ID using just the fourth cell and the netmask 255.255.255.0. Now, when the node receives packets, it immediately discards any that do not match its network ID.

Routing

When subnets are connected to an Internet, IP gateways and routers are used to forward only the essential packets to their respective destinations, and to discard the rest. They act as filters to separate network traffic. When a node wants to communicate with a node with a different network ID, a gateway advances the packet to the appropriate destination network.

A gateway typically has two or more adapters. Each is connected to a separate LAN and is running some sort of routing software to facilitate the forwarding. When you set up a node, you must specify the default gateway, the latter which is essentially a router. If this gateway goes down, communication with nodes having other network IDs is not possible.

Installing TCP/IP Support

Because the TCP/IP protocol is the most accepted and complete transport mechanism in the world, Microsoft decided to support it natively in Windows NT. For the user, this means that using TCP/IP to communicate with other computers requires no additional software. Other products produced by third-party developers might enhance the functionality of TCP/IP on your Windows NT network, but the tools already provided enable you to connect to systems running Windows NT, to other Microsoft networking products, and to non-Microsoft systems such as Unix.

You can install the TCP/IP components of Windows NT when you first set up your system or later as you expand your network. This section assumes you have already installed Windows NT on a machine and are adding TCP/IP functionality.

 You must be logged in as Administrator or as a member of the Administrator's group to install and configure all the elements of TCP/IP mentioned in this chapter.

To install the TCP/IP protocol and utilities on your Windows NT server, perform the following steps:

1. Open the Control Panel and double-click on the Networks icon. The Network Settings dialog box appears (see fig. 5.5).

2. Click on the Add **S**oftware button to open the Add Network Software dialog box (see fig. 5.6).

3. Scroll through the list of network software components until you see the option TCP/IP Protocol and related components. Choose the option, then click on the Continue button.

Figure 5.5

*The Network Settings
dialog box.*

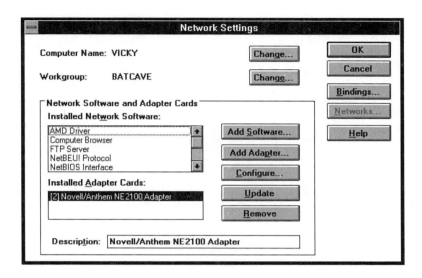

Figure 5.6

*The Add Network
Software dialog box.*

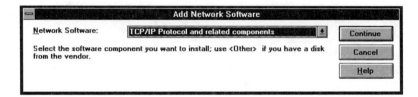

4. The Windows NT TCP/IP Installation Options dialog box that appears includes a number of different components (see fig. 5.7). You might want to install all of them eventually, but for now, select only TCP/IP Internetworking, Connectivity Utilities, and Simple TCP/IP Services.

The dialog box shows how much disk space each component requires. You should have plenty of room for all the components you selected. To see the space required for all the components you selected and the space available on your hard drive, look at the values below the Components box. If you were to install all the components, you would need about 2 MB of free disk space.

5. Click on the Continue button; Windows NT starts copying the necessary files.

TCP/IP Installation Options

Table 5.1 describes each of the components from the Windows NT TCP/IP Installation Options dialog box in more detail.

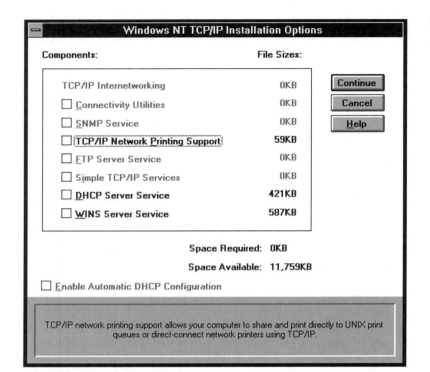

Figure 5.7

The Windows NT TCP/IP Installation Options dialog box.

Table 5.1 TCP/IP Components and Their Descriptions

Component	Description
TCP/IP Internetworking	This option is chosen automatically. In other words, if you are installing any TCP/IP software, you also are installing the software associated with this choice. It includes the TCP/IP protocol itself and the TCP/IP utilities, the Windows Sockets interfaces, and the ability to run NetBIOS over TCP/IP.
Connectivity Utilities	The next component, and the first real option, is Connectivity Utilities. This includes all the connectivity commands, such as ftp, finger, lpr, rcp, rexec, rsh, telnet, and tftp. It also includes the diagnostic utilities, such as arp, hostname, ipconfig, lpq, nbtstat, netstat, ping, route, and tracert.

Component	Description
SNMP Service	This option is useful if you plan to manage this station with an SNMP monitor like Sun Net Manager or HP Open View. Installing this option also gives you the ability to monitor TCP/IP statistics using Performance Monitor. Performance Monitor is a tool included with Windows NT that gathers statistics and sets alarms for certain system components. It can be very helpful in telling you whether or not your server is overworked.
TCP/IP Network Printing Support	With this component installed, you can print to TCP/IP printers on the network, including Unix print queues or TCP/IP-enabled printers connected directly to the network. In addition, if you want to use the Lpdsvr service so that Unix systems can print to Windows NT printers, you must install this component.
FTP Server Service	This is the software that enables clients on the Internet to copy files to or from your system. Depending on what type of Internet server you intend to configure your Windows NT machine for, you might want to install this option.
Simple TCP/IP Services	Selecting this component installs the client software necessary for the Character Generator, Daytime, Discard, Echo, and Quote of the Day services. If you have other computers on your network that support these protocols, installing the Simple TCP/IP Services enables your Windows NT machine to respond.
DHCP Server Service	DHCP stands for Dynamic Host Configuration Protocol, a protocol that automatically assigns IP addresses and provides management of those addresses. When you select this option, you are installing the server portion of the software. The client software must be installed on each workstation on your network. Since Internet hosts have static IP addresses, you do not need to install this portion when making your Windows NT Internet server. If this server is to be accessed through TCP/IP from other clients on the local network, however, then you might need to install it. Chapter 6, "IP Addressing and Configuration," discusses DHCP in greater detail.

continues

Component	Description
WINS Server Service	WINS stands for Windows Internet Name Service. The Internet in this name, however, is different than the Internet to which you are trying to connect. WINS is actually a naming service, much like DNS, that resolves names and their associated IP addresses. When you select this option, you are making your machine a WINS server capable of handling name registrations, queries, and releases of IP addresses. This service works well for networks also using DHCP, but is ineffective on the Internet. If this server will be accessed through TCP/IP from other clients on the local network, then you might want to install it. Chapter 6 discusses WINS in greater detail.
Enable Automatic DHCP Configuration	This feature installs the client portion of the DHCP software on your Windows NT computer. It is not available for selection if you have installed the DHCP Server or WINS Server services. Because you are configuring your machine to be an Internet server, you do not want to enable this option. You need to create a static IP address on your machine—you have no use for dynamic IP address configuration.

If you need more information concerning any of these items, read the hint bar at the bottom of each TCP/IP dialog box. The Help feature also offers more detailed information. Click on its button for assistance.

Basic TCP/IP Configuration

After the TCP/IP software has been copied to your Windows NT computer, you need to provide some configuration information. First, Windows NT asks for a valid IP address. For now, you need to insert the IP address information manually. In the TCP/IP Configuration dialog box, enter your machine's IP address, the subnet mask, and the default gateway (see fig. 5.8). The section of the box that deals with WINS is covered later in this chapter. Leave it blank for now.

 If your network is already running TCP/IP, make sure that you get a valid IP address from your network administrator. Otherwise, you might accidentally choose an address used elsewhere on the network, causing all sorts of problems.

If you are confused about any part of this dialog box, remember that components are explained in the hint bar. More detailed information is available if you click on the Help button.

Figure 5.8

The TCP/IP Configuration dialog box.

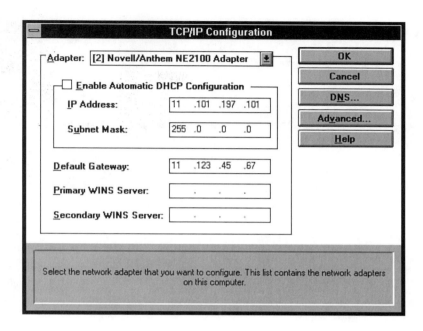

Figure 5.8

The TCP/IP Configuration dialog box.

Configuring TCP/IP for DNS

On the right side of the TCP/IP Configuration dialog box is a button labeled D<u>N</u>S. The *Domain Name System* (DNS) is a naming service popular in Unix networks and on the Internet. It provides a means of resolving system names with IP addresses. If you have a DNS server on your network and want to use its naming services, Windows NT gives you this option (see fig. 5.9).

The DNS Configuration dialog box is split into three sections. In the uppermost section, you tell Windows NT which naming resources you want to search first. If you have a HOSTS file on your machine, Windows NT can use that in conjunction with the DNS server. You can configure TCP/IP to search either resource first.

In the middle section of the DNS Configuration dialog box, you insert the DNS server's IP address. You can include up to three IP addresses, but keep in mind that the order in which they are listed in this box is the order Windows NT uses to query the name servers. You should, therefore, list first the DNS server you use most often (if there is one). Use the arrow buttons at the right of the box to change the order.

In the third section in the DNS Configuration dialog box, you can list domain suffixes. This list specifies the DNS domain suffixes to be appended to host names during name resolution. You can add up to six entries in this list. The domain suffixes are used with the host names to create a *fully qualified domain name* (FQDN). An FQDN consists of the host name, followed by a period, followed by the domain name. If *editorial* is the host name, for example, and *lantimes.com* is the domain name, the FQDN is *editorial.lantimes.com*.

You can set up a Windows NT server as a DNS server by installing the software provided in the Windows NT 3.5 Resource Kit. If you do not plan to have a DNS server of your own, contact your service provider for the IP address of their DNS server.

If you have a small network, it probably is easier to use the DNS server maintained by your Internet service provider. Most providers are willing to maintain your domain information for a fee. You want to provide your own DNS server if you have your own domain on the Internet, or if you want to access DNS from your own LAN rather than going through your Internet provider.

When you have filled in all the information necessary in the DNS Configuration dialog box, click on OK to return to the TCP/IP Configuration dialog box.

Configuring Advanced TCP/IP Options

Depending on the complexity of your TCP/IP network, you might want to configure the Advanced TCP/IP Options of Windows NT. To do so, click on the Advanced button in the TCP/IP Configuration dialog box. The Advanced Microsoft TCP/IP Configuration dialog box appears (see fig. 5.10). At the top of the box, you can select the network adapter for which you want to configure specific options. If you have only one adapter, then this does not affect to you; but if you have two or more adapters, some of the options in this dialog box are of special interest.

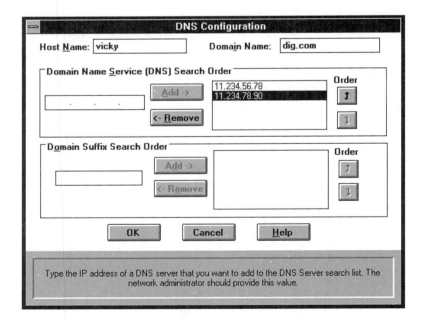

Figure 5.9

The DNS Configuration dialog box.

Figure 5.10

*The Advanced Microsoft
TCP/IP Configuration
dialog box.*

Advanced Microsoft TCP/IP Configuration

Adapter: [2] Novell/Anthem NE2100 Adapter

IP Address:

IP Addresses: 11.101.197.101 / Subnet Masks: 255.0.0.0

SubnetMask:

Default Gateway: 11.123.45.67

Add ->
<- Remove

Windows Networking Parameters

☐ Enable DNS for Windows Name Resolution
☒ Enable LMHOSTS Lookup   Import LMHOSTS...
Scope ID:

☐ Enable IP Routing
☐ Enable WINS Proxy Agent

OK   Cancel   Help

Type additional IP addresses for the selected network adapter.

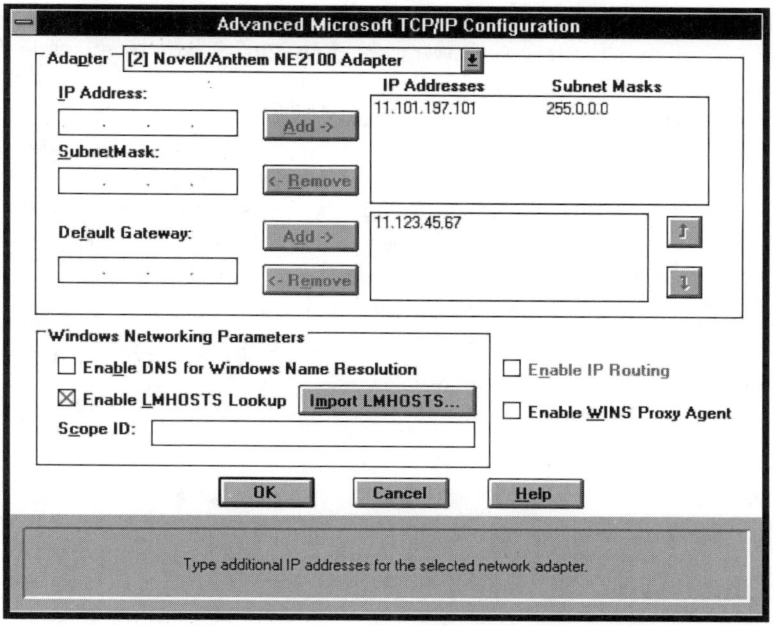

Below the Adapter setting is a section of the box in which you can add IP addresses and subnet masks to your machine. You can configure up to five IP addresses for each network adapter on your system. This feature comes in handy if you happen to run multiple IP networks on the same physical segment.

You also can define up to five default gateways for the selected adapter to use. As with the list of DNS servers, the order in which the gateways are listed is important. Windows NT searches the gateway at the top of the list first, and then on down the line.

Two other options deal specifically with Windows networking parameters. Normally, DNS servers are used in host-based TCP/IP environments like Unix

networks or the Internet. If you select the box next to the option Enable DNS for Windows Name Resolution, then you can use a DNS server to resolve naming requests for Windows networks also.

An LMHOSTS file provides another way to resolve naming requests on a Windows network. Similar to a HOSTS file, LMHOSTS resolves addresses with NetBIOS names. If you aren't familiar with the function of LMHOSTS files, don't worry—Chapter 6 covers the concept in detail. The Advanced Microsoft TCP/IP Configuration dialog box also gives you the option of importing an LMHOSTS file.

The next option in this section of the dialog box enables you to enter a Scope ID. A *scope ID* provides a way to group a set of computers so that they only communicate with each other. If you enter a scope ID in this field, your computer will be able to communicate only with other computers on your network that have the exact same scope ID. Usually, you want to leave this value blank.

Finally, you have the option in the Advanced Microsoft TCP/IP Configuration dialog box to enable IP routing. This option is available to you only if you have two network adapters configured for the TCP/IP protocol with their own IP addresses. The WINS Proxy agent field applies only if you have a WINS server on your network.

Configure the options you want to change, then click on OK to return to the TCP/IP Configuration dialog box.

Configuring TCP/IP for Remote Access

Many Windows NT users install *Remote Access Service* (RAS) so they can use their network from a remote site. This remote access is available for TCP/IP networks as well. Remote users can dial in to a RAS server and have complete access to the Internet, as if they were physically connected to the network through a LAN adapter.

RAS, however, has some special considerations in a TCP/IP network. How do users resolve naming and address queries, for example—through the RAS server on the LAN or through the remotely attached computer connected with a phone line? To configure RAS for use on TCP/IP networks, you first need to run the RAS setup program (see fig. 5.11). To get there, perform the following steps:

1. Open the Networks icon from the Control Panel.

2. Select Remote Access Service from the list, and click the **C**onfigure button. If you haven't already installed Remote Access Service support, you need to add the software first.

3. In the Remote Access Setup dialog box, click on the **N**etwork button to open the Network Configuration dialog box (see fig. 5.12).

4. From the Server Setting section of this dialog box, select TC**P**/IP and click on the C**o**nfigure button next to it. (If TCP/IP is already installed on your system, that box is checked by default.)

   The RAS Server TCP/IP Configuration dialog box appears (see fig. 5.13).

The RAS Server TCP/IP Configuration dialog box enables you to configure the IP address allocation for remote clients using RAS. You can configure remote users so that they get their IP addresses either from a DHCP server or from a static IP address pool. If you have a DHCP server on your network, you can use that option. But if you do not use such a server, select the Use **s**tatic address pool option.

Figure 5.11

The Remote Access Setup dialog box.

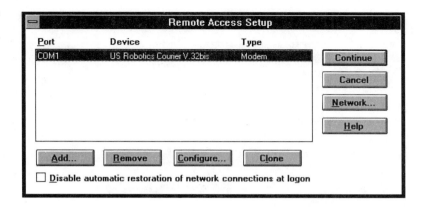

Figure 5.12

The Network Configuration dialog box.

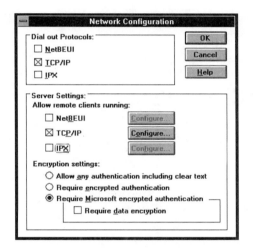

If you select the second option, you need to enter a valid range of IP addresses for remote users. If you want, you also can exclude a range of addresses that remote clients should not have. Simply enter the addresses in the appropriate fields, then add them to the list. To remove them, highlight the range in the Excluded ranges box and click on the Remove button.

All of these instructions assume that the RAS server assigns the IP address. A RAS client, however, can request its own specific address. To enable this option, select the check box at the bottom of the dialog box. If a remote client can request its own IP address, it also can request a specific DNS or WINS server for name resolution.

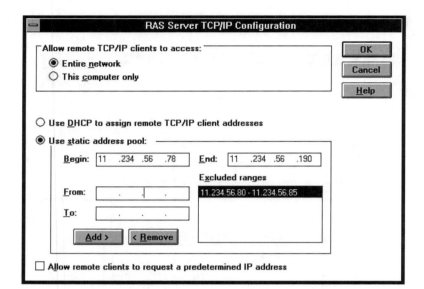

Figure 5.13

The RAS Server TCP/IP Configuration dialog box.

Basic TCP/IP Utilities

Windows NT includes many TCP/IP utilities, including telnet, ftp, finger, rcp, rexec, rsh, lpr, and tftp. These applications provide users with access to resources on non-Microsoft hosts, such as Unix. They are important when setting up your Windows NT server on the Internet because most of the Internet servers are Unix based. Windows NT also includes a suite of TCP/IP diagnostic tools, including arp, hostname, ipconfig, nbtstat, netstat, ping, lpq, tracert, and route.

In addition to these TCP/IP utilities, your Windows NT operating system also includes services that make your server Internet ready—you don't have to purchase any additional software. Examples of these services include the FTP Server service, WINS for name resolution, and DHCP service for the dynamic IP addressing of servers and clients. The next three sections will focus on some of these TCP/IP tools which are available in Windows NT.

ping

The first utility you probably should try is ping. ping sends a packet to the destination server and waits for an acknowledgment. Windows NT's ping sends four packets, giving you an idea as to the health of your line. If just one packet is tried and it fails, it could just be due to line noise along the wire. If two or three packets fail, but the others return, you know that your configuration is probably intact, but the medium is having some problems. If all four packets are acknowledged, then you know you have a fairly stable connection.

If you aren't having any luck getting acknowledgments from the other servers, try typing **ping localhost**. This command sends a packet to your own server. The IP address 127.0.0.1 is reserved for a localhost connection. If everything is configured correctly, you should see the replies. If not, then you know the protocol is not configured properly or is not bound to a network adapter.

FTP

One of the first reasons people started connecting to the Internet (or to any network, for that matter) was to share files. The file transfer protocol (FTP) still handles most of the file transfer traffic. This utility can be used to list directories, copy files to and from an FTP server, and even to translate some files.

Two parts to FTP must be present for it to work—a client portion and a server portion. Windows NT includes both tools, depending on whether you want to be a server or client on an internetwork. Both, however, can work simultaneously.

The FTP server on Windows NT runs as a service. This means it starts when the machine boots; no one must necessarily be logged in to start it. You can start and stop the service using the Services application in the Control Panel.

Telnet

Telnet is a terminal emulation protocol originally developed for ARPAnet. It enables users to interact with any other type of computer in the network. The TCP protocol controls the transfer of the data, and the IP protocol provides the routing mechanisms.

Like FTP, Telnet requires two parts in order for it to work. Windows NT includes the Telnet client. When you install the TCP/IP utilities, note the new icon in the Accessories group. Clicking on this icon opens the Terminal program of Winows NT and initiates the Telnet protocol.

The Telnet server (sometimes called the telnetd for telnet daemon) is not included with Windows NT, but can be obtained by third-party developers.

What NT Does Not Include

Many TCP/IP tools are not included in the base operating system. We talk about many of these tools—the ones necessary to make your computer an Internet server—but be aware, third-party developers provide others. These include X Windows, NFS, routed, telnetd, and other enhanced connectivity applications.

Connectivity with third-party products usually is accomplished through support of the Windows Sockets *Application Programming Interface* (API). Developers use this network API to create products for the Windows and Windows NT operating systems. It was designed to provide a standard of compatibility with Windows-based TCP/IP utilities.

Windows NT supports 32-bit Windows Sockets compliant applications. Windows NT also provides compatibility, however, for applications written with 16-bit Windows Sockets. That way, even applications written for standard Windows run without modification on a Windows NT system.

note If you are interested, you can get a copy of the Windows Sockets specification from Microsoft's FTP server on the Internet. The server is called `ftp.microsoft.com`. Text and binary versions of the specs are located in the `\bussys\winsock\spec11` directory.

Summary

The basic protocol on the Internet is TCP/IP. Microsoft includes support for TCP/IP in the base Windows NT system. You also can use RAS to initiate a TCP/IP connection over PPP or SLIP. TCP/IP must be configured with a valid IP address, a default gateway (router), and a DNS server. You can set up a gateway or DNS server using Windows NT machines or other hardware. Many TCP/IP applications are included with Windows NT, but many are only available from third-party developers. Most of the third-party developers, however, are working on TCP/IP client applications for Windows NT. The Internet server applications are available as freeware or shareware and are included with this book.

6

IP Addressing and Configuration

I f you plan to connect your whole network to the Internet, then every host and client on your network must have its own unique IP address. Keeping track of IP addresses on a network can be one of the network manager's biggest problems. Windows NT includes some tools that make it easy to manage IP addresses on a large network. These tools—Domain Host Configuration Protocol (DHCP) and Windows Internet Naming Service (WINS)—automatically and dynamically allocate IP addresses to clients.

These tools not only are helpful from a management perspective, they also can aid the mobile user who might log in to several networks through the *local area network* (LAN) or *Remote Access Service* (RAS). This chapter discusses these special features, as well as HOSTS and LMHOSTS files of Windows NT.

Using DHCP

Administrators who manage and maintain a TCP/IP network most often complain about the difficulty in keeping track of all the addresses and names. *Domain Name Service* (DNS) servers alleviate some of the frustration by giving clients a central location in which to look for names and addresses. DNS servers actually map host names to their appropriate addresses. However, they fail to solve one problem—DNS servers are not dynamic.

As TCP/IP networking becomes more prevalent, IP addresses become less available. This problem is due to the limited pool of addresses available; the IP address pool is quickly being depleted because of the increased number of users requesting IP addresses for Internet access. Although many of the IP addresses assigned to machines on your network are used perhaps only sporadically, those addresses are dedicated.

DHCP is designed to solve this problem and to simplify TCP/IP network administration. A DHCP server makes assigning addresses to machines a dynamic process rather than a static one. The Internet Engineering Task Force (IETF) designed DHCP as an extension of the *Bootstrap Protocol* (BOOTP).

 Protocols such as the DHCP and BOOTP enable the use of centralized servers to hand out **t i p** unique IP addresses and other configuration information on an as-needed basis.

Typically, a new user on the network applies to the manager for a valid IP address. The manager makes an entry in the HOSTS tables or DNS database. That user might only need that address occasionally or even temporarily; however, while the address is assigned to a machine, no one else can use it.

DHCP automatically assigns IP addresses as needed and then releases them when they are no longer necessary. A DHCP server has a pool of valid addresses it can assign to clients. When a client's system starts, the DHCP client sends a message on the network requesting an address.

Each DHCP server (several can exist) replies with an IP address and configuration information. The DHCP client collects the servers' offers and selects a valid address, sending the confirmation back to the offering DHCP servers. Each DHCP server receives the confirmation from the client. The DHCP server with the address the client selected sends an acknowledgment message back to the client. All the other DHCP servers rescind their earlier offers and put the offered address back into their pool. After the client receives the acknowledgment message from a DHCP server, that client can participate in the TCP/IP network.

The DHCP server essentially leases the address to the client. That lease can have time limits so that unused addresses are automatically returned to the address pool. However, if the lease expires, but the machine is still using the address, the DHCP server can renew the lease so that the client can continue with the same address.

 You can install DHCP on the machine serving as your Internet server or on any other Windows NT server on the network. Depending on the loads your Internet server carries, you might want to offload DHCP and WINS to another, less busy machine.

Installing DHCP

To install a DHCP server on a Windows NT machine, go to the TCP/IP Installation Options dialog box.

1. Double-click on the Network icon in the Control Panel.

2. Choose Add Software.

3. Select the TCP/IP Protocol and Related Components option in the software list.

4. Select the DHCP Server Service from the list and click on OK.

Windows NT copies the necessary files to your hard disk.

Configuring DHCP

To configure the DHCP Server services, you must use the DHCP Administrator utility. This utility is automatically installed when you install the DHCP services. Double-click on the DHCP Administrator icon in the Network Administration group to activate the DHCP Manager dialog box. Figure 6.1 shows the DHCP Administrator (or Manager) utility.

Creating a Scope

The first thing you want to do in terms of configuration is to create a DHCP administrative scope. A scope is equivalent to a subnet on your network (see Chapter 5, "Understanding TCP/IP," for information on subnetting). Highlight the Local Machine entry under the DHCP Servers list. Choose Scope, Create from the menu; the Create Scope dialog box appears (see fig. 6.2).

Figure 6.1

The DHCP Manager dialog box.

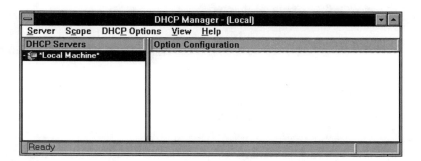

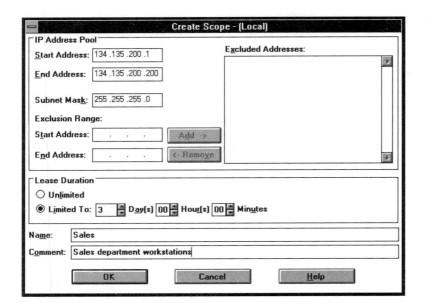

Figure 6.2

*The Create Scope
dialog box.*

In this dialog box, you define the pool of addresses DHCP dynamically makes available to DHCP clients. Enter the start and end addresses to define the range. If you want to exclude some addresses that are in that pool, you can enter either an excluded range or an excluded address. To insert an excluded range, enter values in the Start Address and End Address fields. To exclude a single address, enter the address in the Start Address field. The excluded ranges and addresses should include other DHCP servers, non-DHCP clients, diskless workstations, and RAS clients.

As you insert excluded ranges or addresses, click on the Add button to add them to the list on the right. If you make a mistake or change your mind about an excluded address, highlight it and click on the Remove button.

The next section of the Create Scope dialog box—called Lease Duration—governs the length of time DHCP clients are allowed to keep their addresses. Remember, the capability to assign and release addresses dynamically provides one of the main reasons for installing a DHCP server.

If you want your DHCP server to assign addresses as they are requested, without releasing them, click on the Unlimited button. More than likely, however, you want to define a duration of a few days or hours. If you specify a duration of three days (the default value), the DHCP server waits three days, then checks to see if the client is still using that address. If so, the lease can be renewed.

If you have a shortage of valid IP addresses on your network and machines connect and disconnect quite frequently at will, three days might be too long for a lease. You might want to specify only a few hours. The only problem with this specification, however, is the added traffic of frequently negotiating addresses between DHCP servers and DHCP clients.

If you have plenty of IP addresses for your network, yet still want to free unused addresses after a specific time period, it might be more appropriate to assign a longer lease duration, such as 30 days.

The only other information you need to enter in the Create Scope dialog box is a scope name. The name can be up to 128 characters and can be anything the user wants it to be. It can include letters, numbers, and hyphens. Any other information you want to include about the scope can be entered in the Comment field.

When you finish entering all the values in the dialog box, choose OK. Windows NT tells you on the

screen that the scope has been successfully created, but is not yet activated. Here in the dialog box, you have the option of activating it. Choose Yes if you want to do so.

t i p If you ever need to change the scope properties, highlight the scope on the left side of the DHCP Manager utility and choose Scope, Properties.

Viewing Active Leases

Also from the Scope menu, you can select Active Leases to see which computers are using your DHCP server. The Active Leases dialog box appears (see fig. 6.3). Highlight a client and choose Properties to see the IP address, when the lease expires, the client name, and the Client Identifier—usually the media access control (MAC) address of the network adapter on that machine.

Figure 6.3

The Active Leases dialog box.

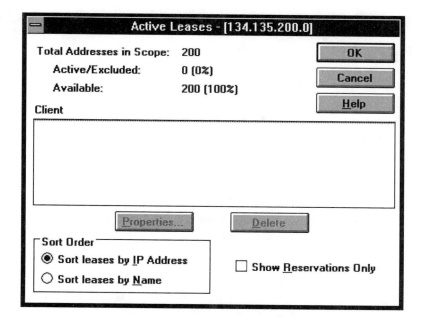

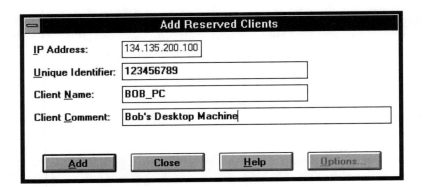

Figure 6.4

The Add Reserved Clients dialog box.

Reserving Addresses

Choose the Add Reservations option to activate the Add Reserved Clients dialog box, in which you can reserve a specific address for a specific client (see fig. 6.4). You can specify any unused IP address from the address pool. In the Unique Identifier field, enter the MAC address of the network adapter on the client computer.

Next, fill in the computer name for the client receiving the reserved address. You do not have to enter the exact computer name for the client. Put any other information you want to enter about the client in the Client Comment field.

Changing Configuration Parameters

The DHCP Manager utility enables you to change the configuration parameters the server assigns to its clients. The options have default values based on standard parameters defined by the Internet Networking Group in RFC 1542. You can change these parameters to affect every client the DHCP Server services, or clients in a certain scope.

You also can change the default values themselves. These TCP/IP networking options are advanced, and

unless you know exactly what you are doing, you can degrade performance or make the DHCP Server unusable.

Using WINS

A Windows Internet Naming Service (WINS) server maintains a database of computers and their associated IP addresses. It provides dynamic name resolution support, and therefore, is suited to work in conjunction with DHCP servers rather than the typical DNS server, the latter of which WINS does not recognize. In fact, when dynamic address changes are made through DHCP for computers that move between subnets, those changes are automatically made in the WINS database.

Installing WINS

Like the DHCP software, WINS has server and client components. WINS name resolution is automatically installed and configured for you when you install DHCP. If you have yet to enable DHCP and want to check out WINS, you need to install WINS manually. To do so, perform the following steps:

1. Double-click on the Network icon in the Control Panel.

2. Choose Add Software to activate the Network Software Installation dialog box.

3. Select TCP/IP Protocol and Related Components from the list.

4. Click on the Continue button.

5. Choose WINS Server Service.

6. Click on Continue; Windows NT copies the necessary files to your hard disk.

When you install WINS, Windows NT adds a utility called WINS Manager to the Network Administration group. Use this tool to manage your WINS server.

On the left side of the WINS Manager application window is a list of WINS servers (see fig. 6.5).

As you highlight a WINS server with your mouse, statistics about that server appear on the right side of the window. Table 6.1 explains what these statistics mean.

If you want to clear the statistics in this table, choose View, Clear Statistics. Because the Statistics table does not dynamically update itself, you might want to refresh the numbers occasionally when the WINS Manager is open. To do so, choose View, Refresh Statistics, or press F5.

To add WINS servers to your WINS Manager list, choose Server, Add WINS Server. Windows NT then prompts you to enter the IP address of the WINS server you want to add. To delete a server from the WINS Manager list, choose Server, Delete WINS Server.

Figure 6.5

The WINS Manager dialog box.

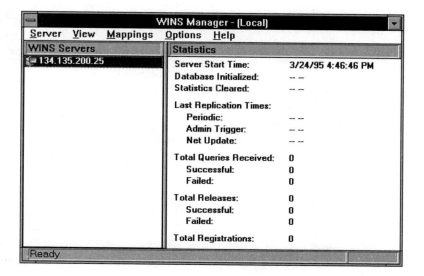

Table 6.1   Statistics in WINS Manager

Statistic	Meaning
Total Queries Received	The number of name query request messages received by this WINS server
Total Releases	The number of messages received that indicate a NetBIOS application has shut itself down
Total Registrations	The number of name registration requests accepted by this WINS server

Setting Up a WINS Replication Partner

Keeping the WINS database on one server does not make sense. If that server goes down, someone else needs to handle name resolution on the network. For this reason, consider creating a replication partner for your WINS server. A *replication partner* helps ensure that the database is always available and also helps balance the job of keeping the database current among more machines.

To set up a replication partner, choose Server, Replication Partners; the Replication Partners dialog box appears (see fig. 6.6). In the WINS Server list, you should see your own local WINS server. To add other WINS servers to the list, choose Add, and enter the address of the WINS server you want to replicate. You can add several WINS servers and set up different relationships with each.

Establishing Relationships between Partners

The relationship that exists between WINS servers is either a Pull or Push relationship. A *Pull Partner* is a WINS server that pulls replicas from its Push Partner. A *Push Partner* is a WINS server that sends

replicas to its Pull Partner. Two WINS servers can be both Push and Pull Partners with each other.

Because of the extra traffic, you probably do not want the database to replicate every time an entry is made. Click on the Configure buttons under Replication Options to define when and how often the WINS servers share data.

You can configure other aspects of your WINS server by choosing Server, Configuration. You can adjust the parameters listed in table 6.2.

You also can configure Push and Pull parameters of your WINS server. If you want your WINS server to pull replication information when the server initializes, choose Initial Replication. If the servers do not respond immediately, you also can insert a Retry Count.

For Push Partners, have your WINS server inform them of the database status when the system is initialized or when an address changes in a mapping record. This can be accomplished by choosing the option available for this purpose. When you are done configuring the options in this dialog box, choose OK.

Figure 6.6

The Replication Partners dialog box.

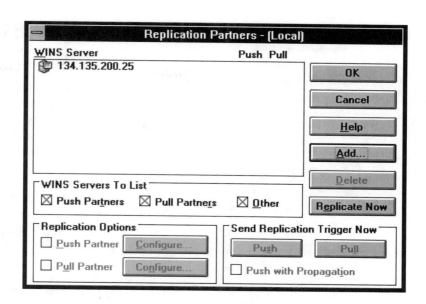

Table 6.2 WINS Server Configuration

Configuration Option	Meaning
Renewal Interval	Specifies how often a client reregisters its name. The default is 96 hours.
Extinction Interval	Specifies the interval between when an entry is marked released and when it is marked extinct. The default is 96 hours.
Extinction Timeout	Specifies the interval between when an entry is marked extinct and when the entry is finally scavenged from the database. The default is 96 hours.
Verify Interval	Specifies the interval after which the WINS server must verify that old names it does not own are still active. The default is 20 times the extinction interval.

To see a copy of the WINS database, choose Mappings, Show Database. The Show Database dialog box appears, in which you can see host names and the addresses to which they are mapped (see fig. 6.7). Sort the database whichever way makes it easiest to find information.

Additionally, you can configure this dialog box to show all the mappings in the database or only mappings that relate to a specific WINS server. If you want to view only mappings related to a specific host, use the Set Filter option to weed unwanted entries from the list.

Your local WINS database should periodically be cleared of unwanted entries. Sometimes entries are registered at another WINS server but are not cleared from the local database. The process of clearing unnecessary entries from the database is called *scavenging,* and can be carried out by choosing Mapping, Initiate Scavenging.

Using HOSTS and LMHOSTS Files

Although you probably want to use DNS or DHCP and WINS for name resolution on your TCP/IP Windows NT network, you also should be aware of a couple of other options Windows NT offers to resolve host names.

TCP/IP for Windows NT uses two text files to resolve host names with their respective addresses. Both files are found in the \WINNT\SYSTEM32 \DRIVERS\ETC directory. One is the HOSTS file; the other is the LMHOSTS file.

Understanding HOSTS Files

If you have any experience with TCP/IP networking on Unix or any other platform, you probably know what a *HOSTS file* is—a list of IP addresses

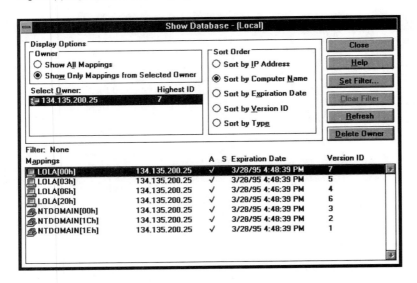

Figure 6.7

The Show Database dialog box.

and host names. If you attempt to use the TCP/IP utilities of Windows NT, you need to specify to which computer you want to attach or log in. You can do so by providing either an IP address, which can be difficult to remember and a pain to type in, or a simple name. If you enabled TCP/IP for Windows NT to use the HOSTS file, it attempts to match the name you type in with an address in the HOSTS file. A HOSTS file is the easiest way to resolve names on a TCP/IP network.

Table 6.3 illustrates what a HOSTS file looks like.

Table 6.3   Sample HOSTS Table

IP Address	Server Name
127.0.0.1	localhost
134.135.200.1	ntserver
134.135.200.102	bruce
134.135.100.100	vicky
134.135.100.150	robin

HOSTS files are easy to set up, but unfortunately, they only work for the computer on which they reside. As your network expands, keeping a current HOSTS file on every computer can be time consuming and problematic.

Understanding LMHOSTS Files

LMHOSTS files have many of the same problems HOSTS files have, but LMHOSTS are more flexible. Like HOSTS, *LMHOSTS* is a simple text file that contains mappings of IP addresses to Windows

NT computer names (which are NetBIOS names). LMHOSTS has greater capabilities than the normal HOSTS file because it enables you to include keywords that tell the TCP/IP components of your Windows NT server how to handle name resolution.

The keywords the LMHOSTS file uses are #PRE, #DOM:*domain*, #INCLUDE *filename*, #BEGIN_ALTERNATE, and #END_ALTERNATE. Normally in an LMHOSTS file, anything after the "#" sign is regarded as a remark statement and ignored. If the "#" sign is followed by one of the accepted keywords, however, LMHOSTS treats the statement as a command. Each of these keywords is explained in the following paragraphs. Refer to the sample LMHOSTS file in the WINNT\ SYSTEM32\DRIVERS\ETC directory for an example.

#PRE following an entry in an LMHOSTS file tells Windows NT to load that entry into the name cache. Loading an entry into cache causes TCP/IP for Windows NT to resolve the name more quickly. When a client tries to associate a name with an IP address, the client first checks the cache memory. If it does not exist there, the client goes to the LMHOSTS file on the hard drive, which is a slower process. Although they take up memory space, you should store the names of servers you access most frequently in cache.

Adding #DOM:*domain* after an entry causes Windows NT to associate that entry with whatever domain you specify. The entry helps Windows NT resolve the names more efficiently because it does not have to search routing tables to find out to which domain the entry belongs.

An #INCLUDE *filename* entry tells your Windows NT machine where to look for other LMHOSTS files that reside on other servers. When entering the file name, use the Uniform Naming Convention (UNC)—that is, two \\ (backward slashes), the machine name, another \, and the file name including directory structure. If, for example, you want to include the LMHOSTS file on Windows NT server desdemona, you specify the file name as follows:

```
#Include
\\DESDEMONA\WINNT\SYSTEM32\DRIVERS\ETC\LMHOSTS.
```

Before a group of multiple #INCLUDE statements, insert the line **#BEGIN_ALTERNATE**. After you enter the statements, insert the line **#END_ALTERNATE**.

The only other special keyword you can use in an LMHOSTS file is \0x*nn*, which is a hexadecimal notation used to support nonprinting characters in NetBIOS names. You probably do not need to use this keyword unless you have an application that uses special names to function properly in routed topologies.

 If you need help creating your HOSTS and LMHOSTS files, see the files themselves in **t i p** the winnt\system32\drivers\etc directory. The files that Windows NT creates when you install TCP/IP connectivity functions contain sample entries and explanations about their use.

Summary

Windows NT includes most of the TCP/IP tools you need. The tools that are missing—like NFS and X Windows support—can be provided by third-party products. Windows NT makes TCP/IP manageable with integrated tools, such as the SNMP agent and the Performance Monitor objects. The DHCP server for address distribution, however, and the WINS server for name resolution combine to provide the best features for managers. These two tools eliminate the biggest headache for TCP/IP administrators—keeping track of the addresses.

p a r t
● ●

Building and Maintaining the Server

7

Installing Server Applications

You can set up a server on the Internet in several ways; but how do you decide which type of server is right for your organization? Each server type has its own strengths, weaknesses, and limitations.

There is nothing wrong with setting up your Windows NT server to perform more than one Internet server task; but be careful. Three problems could possibly creep up when you try to do this.

The first problem is with administration. You may want to make changes to your Web page; but your FTP server is running non-stop, and it's difficult to find a "good" time to make those changes. Making changes to one server application does not necessarily disrupt other applications, but it could potentially.

Another problem arises when you start getting heavy access to your services. One machine, no matter how powerful, might not be able to handle all the traffic you are getting with all the services. The bottleneck may not be the processor, but could easily be the LAN channel. This is hard to judge until you set up your servers and get a feel for what kind of traffic they will have to service.

The final problem is with security. Common sense tells you that the simpler a machine's configuration is, the easier it is to control security. (That's essentially what a *firewall* is—a computer whose sole purpose is to run some sort of routing software— and nothing else.) When you start making a machine more complex by adding more and more software, the chance of security "holes" is greater and greater.

With all that said, however, if you are unsure about what kind of services you want to provide and what kind of traffic the server will have to cater to, starting out with several services on one machine may not be a totally bad idea. Then, as you start to learn what services are getting the most activity, you can offload those to other machines.

The most popular types of Internet servers are FTP and HTTP. This chapter first explains how to set up those. You might, however, want to consider other types. Gopher and WAIS servers help clients find access to your files more easily, so you might want to incorporate those server types into your strategy. You will find instructions on setting up those servers also.

Using FTP Server Services

One of the most commonly used applications in a TCP/IP environment is the *file transfer protocol* (FTP). Windows NT includes an FTP client so that you can initiate file transfers between your machine and another on the network. Windows NT also provides an FTP server so that other machines on the network can initiate file transfers.

Understanding FTP Security Issues

One problem with using FTP Server services on your computer is that unencrypted passwords can cross the network, causing a severe breach in your security. Therefore, you might want to think twice about turning your Windows NT computer into an FTP server.

The security model of the FTP Server service is integrated with Windows NT's own security model. Clients use the Windows NT user accounts and passwords to log into the FTP server through TCP/IP. Access to directories and files on the server is maintained by Windows NT's security structure as well. For this reason, Microsoft recommends that the FTP Server service be installed on an NTFS partition so that the files and directories made available through FTP can be secured.

Installing FTP Server Services

To install FTP Server services, follow these steps:

1. Choose the Network icon in the Control Panel.

2. In the Network Settings dialog box, click on the Add **S**oftware button. The Add Network Software dialog box appears.

3. Select the TCP/IP Protocol and Related Components entry from the list to bring up the Windows NT TCP/IP Installation options dialog box.

4. Select the **F**TP Server Service option and click OK.

A security warning appears. If you still want to install FTP Server services, click **Y**es. Windows NT copies the appropriate files.

Configuring FTP Services

After the FTP server software is installed on your computer, the FTP Service dialog box appears on your screen (see fig. 7.1). Here you can configure such items as maximum connections and idle timeout periods. You also can specify the home directory FTP clients default to when they first connect.

Another part of this configuration box enables you to configure anonymous connections. If you want, users can log into your FTP Server service with the username Anonymous. The password is the user account name. By default, the Anonymous account has the same rights and privileges on the Windows NT system as user Guest, but you can change that if you want. You can create a user profile using the User Account Editor of Windows NT to create a

default Anonymous user with whatever rights you choose and enter that user name in the appropriate field.

 n o t e If for some reason you have a username Anonymous on your Windows NT system and that user logs into your FTP server, she will receive permissions based on the Guest account, not the native Anonymous account.

You can set your FTP server to accept Anonymous connections only. If security is an important issue in your network, yet you still want to enable FTP Server services, then perhaps you should select this option. That way, the only passwords that need to travel the wire unencrypted are the usernames of the people logging in with the Anonymous account. To complete the configuration process, click on OK to close the dialog box.

When FTP Server services start, you see a new icon for managing the server in the Control Panel. Double-click on that icon, and the FTP User Sessions dialog box appears. In this box is a list of users connected to your machine through FTP. You can see the usernames, IP addresses they are connecting from, and how long they have been connected. If they logged in using the Anonymous account, you can see the passwords they used. You can disconnect all of them if you need to by clicking on the Disconnect **A**ll button at the bottom of the dialog box.

While the box is open, click on the **S**ecurity button to see the level of security that FTP initiates on its own—independent of the Windows NT security architecture. The FTP Server Security dialog box appears (see fig. 7.2).

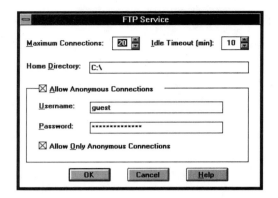

Figure 7.1

The FTP server configuration dialog box.

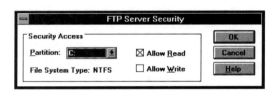

Figure 7.2

Setting FTP Server security.

The FTP Server Security dialog box enables you to configure each partition on your system for Read and Write access. One way to add an extra level of security to your system for FTP clients is to place all sensitive files on a separate partition and grant neither Read nor Write access to that partition. Or if you want to allow users to copy files from your server, but not copy files to your server, select the Allow Read check box and leave the Allow Write check box blank. After you configure the security options for each partition, click on OK.

If you have any questions about the FTP commands that Windows NT uses, select the Windows NT Help icon in the Program Manager Main group. In the Windows NT Help dialog box, click on the Command Reference Help button; then click the FTP commands entry in the Commands dialog box. Click on each FTP command name to see a description of the command as well as valid parameters and syntax.

Using a World Wide Web Server

One of the newest and most exciting uses of the Internet is the World Wide Web, or simply Web, server. Up until now, this book has discussed text-based uses of text-based information. The Web offers much more than that, adding graphics, sound, or video, and the capability to link information on a global scale. Build an interesting Web page, and users will want to visit your site again and again. Build a boring Web page, and it reflects the product you are pedaling. Cruising around the global nets with WWW, following leads, doing research—this is the exhilarating part of "surfing the net."

Understanding the World Wide Web

The World Wide Web hypermedia project was designed and prototyped at CERN (European Laboratory for Particle Physics) in Switzerland. It is based on two elements—the *HyperText Markup Language* (HTML) and the *Uniform Resource Locator* (URL). When used with the *HyperText Transfer Protocol* (HTTP)—Web's server software—there are no boundaries to where you can go or what you can do.

HTML tells the World Wide Web browser (the most common browser are Mosaic and Netscape) how to lay out the text and how to make links to other parts or documents. Making a Web home page can be tedious work. There is still a lot of pain in creating an HTML document, but new tools are coming out every day that make the job easier.

 A *home page* is the first screen a user sees when he accesses your Web server with a browser.

t i p

HTML programming will always be somewhat of an art form. You're often dealing with pictures, and the more interesting things display on the screen, the more traffic you will get of people wanting to take a look.

A *uniform resource locator* (URL) is a system of identifying where a resource resides on the Internet.

You use a URL to point your browser at Web documents anywhere on the Internet. You can also use URLs to link your pages with other pages on other servers.

The URLs don't have to point to HTTP servers either. You can use a URL link in your documents to address FTP servers or Gopher servers. The flexibility of the Web is what makes it so popular.

Organizational Advantages

No matter what your product or service is, you can use a World Wide Web page to educate users. Ever since the creation of the Internet, a company or individual advertising on the Internet through e-mail or newsgroups has been a serious no-no. Try to sell a group on a product, no matter how good, and watch your mailbox fill up with all kinds of *flames* (electronic version of "hate mail").

But you can provide a location for the information and let users come and peruse at their leisure; there is nothing wrong with that. Splatter your home page with any picture you want, and if it's interesting enough, people will want a look.

Besides your home page, one of the first links usually set up on a server is to a What's New section. Guide users through your latest products, your best deals, or your finest stuff, and you get a chance to make an impression.

In fact, you don't even have to have a company that sells a product or service to benefit from setting up a Web site. Many organizations or individuals have created home pages that deal only with their personal interests or hobbies. A Web page exists for almost everything you can imagine.

There are Web sites for the White House, universities, government agencies, or Slovian wine shops. On one hand, it's nice to have the freedom to put whatever you like on your Web page; but on the other hand, realize what you're competing with at the user's end. That's why you should work hard to make your home page as interesting as possible.

Planning Your Web Server

The HTTP software for building a Web server is enclosed with this book. It implements the HTTP/1.0 protocol and runs as a Windows NT "service," just like the FTP server. This version of HTTP originates from the *European Microsoft Windows NT Academic Center* (EMWAC), located at Edinburgh University Computing Service. See the manuals on the companion CD-ROM for more information about this group, including directions on filing bug reports, making suggestions, and so on. Incidentally, if you bought the Windows NT Resource Kit from Microsoft, this is the same software you would get in that kit.

 n o t e Edinburgh University Computing Service will be producing a Professional version of the HTTP server software, which will be marketed through third parties. The version on the CD is free and unsupported; the Professional version will be supported and will have enhanced functionality.

System Requirements

The requirements for this HTTP server are not much different from those of Windows NT itself. That is, you must have the following:

➜ Windows 3.5 final release installed

➜ Microsoft's TCP/IP software installed

➜ At least 16 MB of memory

➜ Network connection—typically Ethernet

Before you install, you should log into your Windows NT server as an Administrator or a user with administrative privileges.

Installing the Web Software

The first thing you need to do is create the directory where you want to install the program, and unzip the file in that directory. Use PKUNZIP, which is available on almost any BBS or online service free of charge. Once unzipped, you should have the files listed in table 7.1.

Table 7.1 HTTP Files and their Descriptions

File	Description
HTTPS.EXE	The HTTP server itself
HTTPS.CPL	The Control Panel applet
HTTPS.HLP	The Control Panel applet help file
HTTPS.DOC	A manual in Word for Windows format
HTTPS.PS	A manual in PostScript format, ready for printing
HTTPS.WRI	A manual in Windows Write format
EGSCRIPT.ZIP	Sample CGI script programs

File	Description
COPYRITE.TXT	The copyright statement for the software
READ.ME	Summary of new features, and so on

You will need to move the HTTPS.EXE file to the \WINNT35\SYSTEM32 directory, where many other services reside. Using the Security/Permissions menu option in the File Manager, verify that the SYSTEM user has read permissions for the file.

Next, move HTTPS.CPL and HTTPS.HLP to the \WINNT35\SYSTEM32 directory. You may want to start the Control Panel to make sure that the HTTP server applet is listed in the Control Panel dialog box.

You might want to check the IP address of your machine. The HTTP server (or any of your IP-based utilities) will not work if this address is wrong. You can do this by typing the following at a command prompt:

HTTPS -IPADDRESS

The machine will display the IP address as reported by the Windows Sockets API.

The next thing you must do is install HTTPS into the table of Windows NT services. This process also registers the service with the Event Logger. To do this, type the following at a command prompt:

HTTPS -INSTALL

After you do this, the system reports success or failure. In the case of failure, consult the online manual by opening or printing one of the manual documents that comes with the software.

After all this is completed, start the Services applet in the Control Panel to verify that the HTTP server is installed and running. Again, if you see any problems, such as the HTTP server program is not running or is missing completely, consult the manual that accompanies the software.

Uninstalling the Software

If you ever need to uninstall the HTTP server software, the following steps show you how it is done:

1. Stop the HTTP Server service by opening the Services applet in the Control Panel and using the Stop button.

2. Type **HTTPS -REMOVE** at a command prompt. This removes the HTTP server from the Service Manager's list of services.

3. Delete the HTTPS.EXE and HTTPS.CPL files from the \WINNT35\SYSTEM32 directory.

Configuration Options

After the HTTP server is installed, configure it with the Control Panel applet. Double-click on the applet, and you see a dialog box like that shown in figure 7.3.

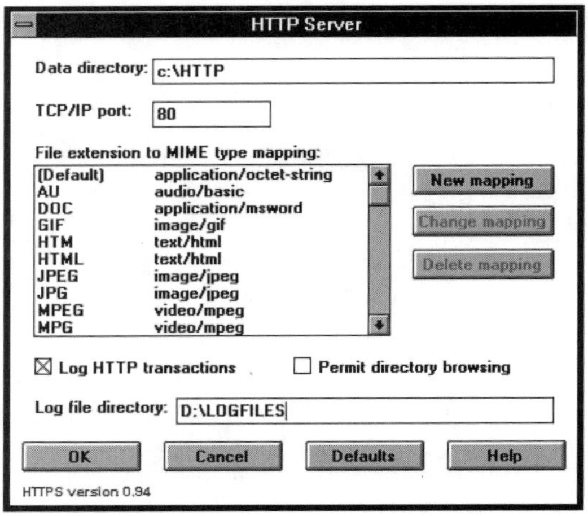

Figure 7.3

The HTTP Server applet.

Note that the version number of the applet is displayed in the lower left-hand corner of the dialog box.

The first thing you want to do is enter a value in the Data Directory field of the dialog box. This directory will be the root of the directory tree containing the files you want to make available on the World Wide Web. Files or directories higher in the file system will not be available to HTTP clients.

When you set up your Web pages, remember that the URLs you set up are relative to this data directory. So if a HTTP client looks for a URL:

```
http://mymachine.mydomain.ac.uk/mydir/myfile.htm
```

The HTTP server sends a file called MYFILE.HTM in the MYDIR subdirectory of the data directory you specify in this field.

Normally, you would point the directory path to a directory on the local machine. However, it is possible to point to a mapped drive on a network server elsewhere. Keep in mind a couple of points, however:

➡ Drive mappings for Windows NT are only established when someone logs into the machine. If no one is logged in, then no mappings are present. Because the HTTP server runs as a Windows NT service, no one needs to be logged in for the HTTP server to service client requests. So if you point the data directory to a network server, make sure that someone has logged in so that the drive letter you specify will be mapped and valid. Otherwise, the drive letter is invalid, and the client cannot access any files.

➡ Drive mappings are specific to a certain user, not the machine itself; so it makes a difference which user is logged in. Make sure that the user account you use to log in has a drive mapping to the server and directory you need—with the same drive letter.

To overcome these problems, you can use the universal naming conventions (UNC) for directory names as opposed to drive mappings. For example, type the following:

`\\servername\sharename`

Of course that directory still has to be a shared resource in the Windows NT system.

From the HTTP Server dialog box, you can also specify the TCP port number on which the HTTP server listens for incoming HTTP connections. The default value for this field is 80, but you can change it to any value that is a positive integer representing a legal and otherwise unused port.

The HTTP server lets you configure multipurpose Internet mail extension (MIME) mappings for your system. The left side of the column represents file-name extensions, and the right column represents the associated MIME type. You can edit, change, or delete these mappings to suit your own needs. Simply select the new mapping button, or highlight a mapping and click on the Change or Delete buttons.

Note that you cannot create a new mapping for a file-name extension already listed in the mapping columns. You must first delete the old mapping; then you can create the new one.

Another field you will see in the HTTP Server dialog box is Log HTTP Transactions. This field is cleared, by default; but if you enable it, the server keeps track of the activity of the server in detail.

It records the time and date of client requests, the IP address of the server and the client, the HTTP command executed, the URL requested, and the version of the HTTP protocol used.

A new file is created every day; the transaction log's file name uses the date a file was created. For example, the file name could be the following:

`HS950630.LOG`

This means that the log file was created June 30, 1995. If you decide to enable this feature, then you should periodically delete old files or move them to another location as they can begin to take up too much disk space on the server.

The location of the log files is defined by the entry in the Log File Directory field of the HTTP Server dialog box. This defaults to the Windows NT installation directory, but you can (and probably should) move it to another location.

The last field you can edit in this dialog box is Permit Directory Browsing. Directory browsing enables a user to navigate through the data directory according to its hierarchical structure. If you don't want users roaming around, then leave this disabled. If you don't mind some browsing, but you don't want a particular subdirectory to be browsable you can create a file called NOBROWSE in it. The existence of this file (it doesn't matter what the contents of the file are) will keep the server from showing this directory's contents.

You can obtain more information about the HTTP server in the manuals that accompany the program files. If you have problems or are looking to further configure your system, please reference one of the online manuals.

Using a Gopher Server

Because so much information to be gathered is on the Internet, it is very easy to be overwhelmed. It's hard to know where to look for the information you are searching for, and there is far too much to sift through. While FTP and Telnet are the most popular means for getting information from other systems, if you don't know exactly what you are looking for and precisely where it is, you will have a hard time finding it.

Gopher was developed to help Internet users to combat this overwhelming feeling as well as to facilitate the search process on the Internet. Named after the mascot of the school that developed the system—the University of Minnesota—Gopher also has connotations associated with the way you use the system—you "go fer" this or you "go fer" that. You can't help but be reminded of the character Gopher on the old television comedy "Love Boat" who knew where to find anything on the ship.

Understanding Gopher

Gopher consists of both server and client programs. It provides an index of information on the Internet. One Gopher server could not, of course, keep up with all the data the Internet holds, but it does not have to. Gopher servers are often interconnected and cross-referenced so that one Gopher server has information and links to other Gopher servers with their information and links, and so on.

With Gopher client software, users do not have to know exactly where certain data or files exist before they go searching for it. All they need to know is the address of a Gopher server, and it presents them with the information they are looking for in a clear, structured, hierarchical list. It does not matter how complex or simple the information a user is looking for.

The software included on this book's CD provides you with the tools you need to set up your Windows NT server as a Gopher server. It runs as a Windows NT service, similar to a daemon that would run in a Unix environment.

This version of Gopher comes from the European Microsoft Windows NT Academic Center (EMWAC) located at Edinburgh University Computing Service. See the manuals on the CD for more information about this group, including directions on filing bug reports, making suggestions, and so on. Incidentally, if you bought the Windows NT Resource Kit from Microsoft, this is the same software you would get in that kit.

 n o t e Edinburgh University Computing Service will be producing a Professional version of the Gopher Server software, which will be marketed through third parties. The version on the CD is free and unsupported; the Professional version will be supported and will have enhanced functionality.

The main reason you will want to set up a Gopher server in your office is to give Internet users a way to find your data easily and effectively.

Planning the Gopher Server

Gopher runs as a service under Windows NT, and the installation is very similar to that of the HTTP server.

System Requirements

The requirements for the Gopher server are not much different from those of Windows NT itself. That is, you must have the following:

→ Windows 3.5 final release installed

→ Microsoft's TCP/IP software installed

→ At least 16 MB of memory

→ Network connection—typically Ethernet

Before you install, you should log into your Windows NT server as an Administrator or a user with administrative privileges.

Installing the Gopher Software

The first thing you need to do is create the directory where you want to install the program, and then unzip the file to that directory. Use the PKUNZIP software. Once unzipped, you should have the files listed in table 7.2.

You need to move the GOPHERS.EXE file to the \WINNT35\SYSTEM32 directory, where many other services reside. Using the Security/Permissions menu option in the File Manager, verify that the SYSTEM user has read permissions for the file.

Next, move GOPHERS.CPL and GOPHERS.HLP to the \WINNT35\SYSTEM32 directory. You may want to start the Control Panel to make sure that the Gopher Server applet is listed in the Control Panel dialog box.

You might want to check the IP address of your machine. The Gopher server (or any of your IP-based utilities) will not work if this address is wrong. You can do this by typing the following at a command prompt:

Table 7.2   Files and their Descriptions

File	Description
GOPHERS.EXE	The Gopher server itself
GOPHERS.CPL	The Control Panel applet
GOPHERS.HLP	The Control Panel applet help file
GOPHERS.DOC	A manual in Word for Windows format
GOPHERS.PS	A manual in PostScript format, ready for printing
GOPHERS.WRI	A manual in Windows Write format
COPYRITE.TXT	The copyright statement for the software
READ.ME	Summary of new features, and so on

GOPHERS -IPADDRESS

The machine displays the IP address as reported by the Windows Sockets API.

The next thing you have to do is to install GOPHERS into the table of Windows NT Services. This process also registers the service with the Event Logger. To do this, type the following at a command prompt:

GOPHERS -INSTALL

After you do this, the system reports success or failure. In the case of failure, consult the online manual by opening or printing one of the manual documents that comes with the software.

After all this is completed, start the Services applet in the Control Panel to verify that the Gopher server is installed and running. Again, if you see any problems, such as the Gopher server program is not running or is missing completely, consult the manual that accompanies the software.

Uninstalling the Software

If you ever need to uninstall the Gopher server software, these steps show you how to do it:

1. Stop the Gopher Server service by opening the Services applet in the Control Panel and using the Stop button.

2. Type **GOPHERS -REMOVE** at a command prompt. This removes the Gopher server from the Service Manager's list of services. This also

deletes the Gopher server's configuration information from the Windows NT Registry.

3. Delete the GOPHERS.EXE and GOPHERS.CPL files from the \WINNT35\SYSTEM32 directory.

Configuration Options

When you double-click on the Gopher Server applet in the Control Panel, a dialog box similar to that shown in figure 7.4 appears.

This dialog box looks very similar to the HTTP Server dialog box discussed in the preceding section. In the first field, you define the data directory to set the root of the directory tree containing the files you want to make available using Gopher.

The same rules apply to specifying a network server in this field as they did with the HTTP Server. If you want to use drive mappings, make sure that someone is logged in to the server, or the drive letter will be invalid. Or use the UNC naming scheme to point to a shared network resource.

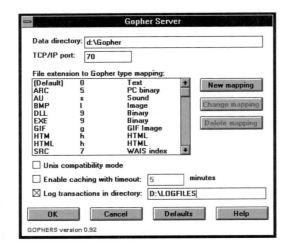

Figure 7.4

The Gopher Server applet.

You can specify the TCP/IP port on which the Gopher Server listens for client requests. The default is 70, but can be any positive integer representing a legal and otherwise unused port.

There is also a table showing the Gopher type mappings. The left column represents the file-name extensions. The center column represents the Gopher types, and the third column lists the associated meanings.

You can edit, change, or delete items in this table with the appropriate buttons. Note that you cannot add an entry with an extension that is already defined. You must either change the mapping, or delete the old mapping first before you create a new one.

If there is no entry in the mapping table for a particular extension, the Gopher Server uses the default extension mapping as defined by the table. This entry may be changed, but never deleted.

The next field in this dialog box is for Unix Compatibility Mode. This is disabled by default. When enabled, the Gopher server recognizes files in the data directory with names that start with a dot. You would only need to enable this option if your data directory pointed to a Unix file system volume. If your data directory is a FAT or NTFS volume, you do not need to enable this option.

The next field is to Enable Caching on the server. To improve performance, the Gopher Server may cache entries in a cache file—titled CACHE.GFR

(or .cache in Unix Compatibility mode). The next time it receives a request involving a similar directory, it reads the information from the cache file.

The cache file should be re-created periodically, or it would never be aware of changes to the files or directories themselves. The default timeout value for the cache file is five minutes. If the server finds a file older than this, it re-creates it. If the timeout value is set to zero, the file is never re-created and must be deleted manually when changes are made.

By default, the Gopher server will not log transactions, but you can enable this feature. The data it records is the time and date of the request, the IP address of the server and the client, and the Gopher selector string sent by the client.

A new log file is created every day, with the date used as part of the file name. Therefore, a file with the following name represents a log file created on June 30, 1995:

GS950630.LOG

You can specify the location where the log files are stored by editing the field in the Gopher server dialog box. This defaults to the Windows NT installation directory, but you can (and probably should) move it to another location.

More information about the Gopher server can be found in the manuals that accompany the program files. If you have problems, or are looking to further configure your system, please reference one of the online manuals.

Using a WAIS Server

Like Gopher, the *Wide Area Information Server*, or WAIS (pronounced "ways"), uses the client server model to navigate around data resources. A WAIS client talks to a WAIS server and asks it to perform a search for data containing a specific word or series of words.

WAIS is based on the Z39.50 standard. Z39.50 is similar to the Structure Query Language (SQL), but is more simple and general. The WAIS server for Windows NT included with this book implements a subset of the Z39.50-88 protocol, with WAIS-specific extensions.

Planning the WAIS Server

WAIS runs as a service under Windows NT, and the installation is similar to that of the HTTP server or the Gopher server.

System Requirements

The requirements for the WAIS server are not much different from those of Windows NT itself. That is, you must have the following:

→ Windows 3.5 final release installed

→ Microsoft's TCP/IP software installed

→ At least 16 MB of memory

→ Network connection—typically Ethernet

You also need to install the WAIS Toolkit files, WAISINDEX.EXE and WAISSERV.EXE. See the next section on the WAIS Toolkit for more details.

Before you install, log in to your Windows NT server as an Administrator or a user with administrative privileges.

Installing WAIS Software

The first thing you need to do is create the directory where you want to install the program, and then unzip the file to that directory. Use the PKUNZIP software. Once unzipped, you should have the files listed in table 7.3.

Table 7.3   Files and their Descriptions

File	Description
WAISS.EXE	The WAIS server itself
WAISS.CPL	The Control Panel applet
WAISS.DOC	A manual in Word for Windows format
WAISS.PS	A manual in PostScript format, ready for printing
WAISS.WRI	A manual in Windows Write format
COPYRITE.TXT	The copyright statement for the software
READ.ME	Summary of new features, and so on

You need to move the WAISS.EXE file to the \WINNT35\SYSTEM32 directory, where many other services reside. Using the Security/Permissions menu option in the File Manager, verify that the SYSTEM user has read permissions for the file.

Next, move WAISS.CPL to the \WINNT35 \SYSTEM32 directory. You may want to start the Control Panel to make sure that the WAIS Server applet is listed in the Control Panel dialog box.

You might want to check the IP address of your machine. The WAIS server (or any of your IP-based utilities) will not work if this address is wrong. You can do this by typing the following at a command prompt:

WAISS -IPADDRESS

The machine displays the IP address as reported by the Windows Sockets API.

Next, you must install WAISS into the table of Windows NT Services. This process also registers the service with the Event Logger. To do this, type the following at a command prompt:

WAISS -INSTALL

After you do this, the system reports success or failure. In the case of failure, consult the online manual by opening or printing one of the manual documents that comes with the software.

After all this is completed, start the Services applet in the Control Panel to verify that the WAIS server is installed and running. Again, if you see any problems, such as the WAIS server program is not running or is missing completely, consult the manual that accompanies the software.

Uninstalling the Software

If you ever need to uninstall the WAIS Server software, these steps show you how to do it:

1. Stop the WAIS Server service by opening the Services applet in the Control Panel and using the Stop button.

2. Type **WAISS -REMOVE** at a command prompt. This removes the WAIS server from the Service Manager's list of services. This also deletes the WAIS server's configuration information from the Windows NT Registry.

3. Delete the WAISS.EXE and WAISS.CPL files from the \WINNT35\SYSTEM32 directory.

Configuration Options

When you start the WAIS Server tool from the Control Panel, the dialog box shown in figure 7.5 appears.

By this time, you should be familiar with the fields in this applet. In fact, it is a lot less complicated than the Gopher server or HTTP server applets.

The first field is for the Data Directory where you specify the root of the directory tree containing the files you want to make available using WAIS. Points in the file system above the data directory or on other disks are not accessible to WAIS clients.

 The data directory on a WAIS server must be located on a disk that uses the high performance file system (HPFS) or NT file system (NTFS) file systems. This is because the indexing process requires long file-name support.

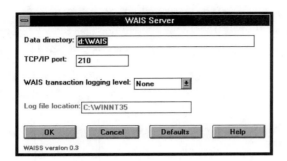

Figure 7.5

The WAIS Server applet.

The data directory can point to a location on a file server, but like the Gopher and HTTP Server, certain points need to be considered. Because a drive mapping is initiated only when someone logs in to the Windows NT machine, you should make sure that someone is logged in when clients begin accessing your WAIS server. Or, use the UNC name for a shared network resource.

You can also define the TCP/IP port for the WAIS server. This is the port that WAIS uses while listening for incoming connections. The default value is 210, but it can be any positive integer representing a legal and otherwise unused port.

Unlike the Gopher and HTTP Server, the WAIS server defines different levels of transaction logging. If you select anything other than None, then for every WAIS request the server receives, it records certain information in the log file.

A new log file is created every day, with the date used as part of the file name. Therefore, a file with the following name represents a file created on June 30, 1995:

WS950630.LOG

You can specify the location where the log files are stored by editing the field in the WAIS Server dialog box. This defaults to the Windows NT installation directory, but you can (and probably should) move it to another location.

More information about the WAIS server can be found in the manuals that accompany the program files. If you have problems, or are looking to further configure your system, please reference the manual.

Using WAISTOOL

This section describes a set of tools for preparing and searching full-text databases for computers running the Windows NT operating system. You should read it if you plan to use the searching capabilities of the Gopher server, the HTTP server, or the WAIS server.

The tools included in this toolkit are listed in table 7.4.

Table 7.4 Tools and their Descriptions

Tool	Description
WAISINDEX	An indexing utility
WAISLOOK	A searching utility
WAISSERV	A Z39.50 protocol handler and search engine

Table 7.5 Files and their Descriptions

File	Description
WAISINDX.EXE	The WAISINDEX program
WAISLOOK.EXE	The searching program
WAISSERV.EXE	The Z39.50 searching program
WAISTOOL.DOC	The manual in Word for Windows format
WAISTOOL.WRI	The manual in Windows Write format
WAISTOOL.PS	The manual in postscript format, ready for printing
READ.ME	Summary of new features, and so on

Using the Windows NT WAIS Toolkit

The WAIS Toolkit is not a service, but a series of applications you will run. To install the toolkit, follow these directions.

System Requirements

To use the Windows NT WAIS Toolkit, you must have the following configuration:

➜ Windows 3.5 final release installed

➜ Microsoft's TCP/IP software installed

➜ At least 16 MB of memory

Before you install, you should log into your Windows NT server as an Administrator or a user with administrative privileges.

Software Installation

The first thing you need to do is create the directory where you want to install the program, and then unzip the file to that directory. Use the PKUNZIP software. Once unzipped, you should have the files listed in table 7.5.

You need to move the EXE files to the \WINNT35\SYSTEM32 directory, where many other services reside. If you are using the NTFS file system, rename the WAISINDX.EXE program to WAISINDEX.EXE. (It is not distributed with that name because of problems when extracting the file to a FAT volume.)

If you have any problems with the files, consult the online manual by opening or printing one of the manual documents that comes with the software.

Uninstalling the Software

If you ever need to uninstall the WAIS server software, simply delete all the files in the preceding table.

Using the Tools

The manual that accompanies the WAIS Toolkit fully explains the use of the tools including syntax and configuration options. That information is not duplicated here; however, this section does offer a brief explanation of the tools.

 WAISINDEX is the utility you use to build and update WAIS databases. Note that this program cannot work with a database on a FAT partition because the intermediate files it creates during the indexing process do not conform to the FAT 8.3 file-name restriction.

The WAISLOOK program is used to search WAIS databases. It is executed automatically by the Gopher and HTTP servers when they need to search a WAIS database, or it can be executed from the console.

WAISSERV is used to search WAIS databases. It is executed automatically by the WAIS server when it receives an incoming call from a WAIS client. It may also be executed manually from the console, but is not particularly useful in this mode.

Summary

You have several options to consider when setting up your Windows NT computer as an Internet server. You must decide what kind of services you want to provide, how much traffic you expect to see, and how much time you want to commit to managing the servers. With the tools provided in the CD-ROM that accompanies this book and the utilities provided with Windows NT, you have all you need to get started building your Windows NT Internet server—whatever server type that might be.

8

Maintaining the Internet Server

Now that you have installed your Internet server, the directions you can take are many. You can keep your system text based, you can make your server available in a graphical format that will ease access and use, or you can use tools to put multimedia directly on the Internet. The answers to many of these decisions become evident as you determine what the stress of your system is. Typical system types are sales, engineering, support, hobby, and social based. Regardless of which avenue you take, you want to consider the security ramifications of each.

If your intended audience is computer literate, maintaining a text-based system is not only very acceptable, but keeps many Internet neophytes away from your data as well. On the other hand, if your desire is to make accessible information to anyone who wants it, consider a graphical interface, such as the World Wide Web. A graphical interface makes your server accessible to anyone.

When all is said and done, the two most basic reasons for setting up an Internet server are to make data available to a large number of system users, and to allow the transferal of information from specified users to specified users (e-mail). Keep these reasons in mind as you determine the type of system you want. You can add bells and whistles 'til your heart's content, but don't lose track of the underlying reasons for undertaking the challenge in the first place.

Realize that when you are linked to the Internet (regardless of what specific form you take), you are in essence an Internet server. This chapter addresses how you present your presence as a full-time Internet server, not how you appear if you are a casual Internet connection (the typical Internet user).

System Stresses

Before you put your system online for others to access, you need to determine what you want to accomplish with your Internet server. Are you a sales-oriented corporation attempting to make data available to your salespeople or resalers? Do you manufacture a product that needs to have updated software or information made available to the people who purchase your equipment? Do you provide technical support that can be taken care of electronically rather than over telephone lines? Do you simply want to develop a hobby- or social-related system for the fun of it?

Whatever your end desires, the more time you put into considering your base needs, the easier it is to get the most from your server.

Sales

If your corporation is a sales-based entity, you want to make available product information for users to review. Data sheets, product specifications, and *white papers* (collection of technical specifications and data) can be made available for anyone to view or download.

You also might want to post questionnaires for those accessing your system. The data collected from these questionnaires can help you determine industry trends or favorability of product paths.

Engineering

A product-development operation has many reasons for making a place for itself on the Internet. The operation can make available beta software to be downloaded by desired users, reducing the cost of physically shipping products by snail mail (the U.S. Postal Service). In addition, the exact time that individual testers download products can be monitored.

You also can post questionnaires for your beta testers to be answered before or after the software is downloaded, forcing those testers to give you feedback concerning different aspects of your software product.

As more companies are decentralizing and contracting out their development, geographical centralization grows increasingly less important. If your developers have some form of online connection to the Internet, updates can be made in real-time (that is, not buffered or delayed), making the development process much more efficient and timely.

You need to make sure your data is protected, especially when product source code is involved. In order for data to transverse the Internet, it must cross servers that are run by people you don't know. Anywhere along the Internet pipeline, between the origination and the destination, data can be monitored. It is always a good idea to incorporate some form of data encryption scheme or device when sending sensitive data to selected persons.

You should segregate specific areas of access with caution in an engineering-based system. Be very selective of who you allow to create or modify the data that you make available to your end users or engineers. Not only is your data at risk of being disabled or corrupted, your company's reputation is at stake as well.

Microsoft, Novell, Santa Cruz Operations, and many, many more companies utilize the Internet for this type of service (Engineering).

Support

Why do numerous technical corporations have a presence on the Internet? The main reason is to provide technical support. Although nothing can take the place of talking directly to a warm body who is knowledgeable and willing to assist you in solving a problem, a support-based forum has proven to be an invaluable companion to a technical support department.

The problem with having to staff a technical support department is that of simple supply and demand. Frequently, calls have to wait in a queue because the number of people requesting assistance is greater than the number of people available to assist. Most calls typically occur between the hours of 8 a.m. and 5 p.m. during normal working days.

One solution is to put in place some vehicle that has no time demands on your limited resources. Complement your normal technical support channels with a technical support forum that is available on the Internet, and your personnel can answer questions as they have time to address them. Further, if you set your technical support Internet system up logically, you can address like questions all at once, which allows your personnel to focus on one topic at a time. You also will find that there are multiple questions that are almost identical, so the act of researching an answer for one question might result in multiple answers.

If you allow your technical support forum to be publicly posted, viewed, and responded to, many of your users will interface with each other and answer their own questions. Obviously, this will relieve much pressure from your official technical support defense line.

Again, Microsoft, Novell, Santa Cruz Operations, and many, many more companies utilize the Internet for this type of service (as a technical support vehicle).

Hobby/Special Interest

Not only can you put an Internet server online for strictly business purposes, you can provide an Internet server that relates to particular hobbies or special interests as well. These types of Internet servers can be quite fun and rewarding to manage. There are servers throughout the Internet that are solely intended for hobbies or special interests, although most servers of this nature are actually subsets of servers that provide other services as well.

 note There are exceptions to this rule, and unfortunately, some of these are software pirate servers that go online during selected times of day and days of the week.

Social

As with the hobby/special interest Internet server, social Internet servers are usually a subset of other full-function Internet servers.

Combined

When you surf the Internet and peruse most university-based Internet services, you undoubtedly will find that university-based server addresses use many combinations of the aforementioned typical server types. Different departments post a variety of data for anyone to review. You also might find areas relating to computers, science, or alternative discussions about popular people or topics (for example, alt.fan.jimmy-buffett). You want your information to conform to generalized classifications that are already in place. The following table defines those classifications:

Classification	Definition
alt	Alternative discussions on various topics
bionet	Biologist interest
bit	A copy of BITNET LISTSERV mailing lists
biz	Business product data, announcements, and so forth
clari	The commercial news service for ClariNet
comp	Computer-related topics and discussions
gnu	GNU-related information
hep	High-energy physics-related information for researchers
ieee	Institute of Electrical and Electronics Engineers-related topics

inet	Another avenue to distribute information for high-volume groups
info	The University of Illinois mailing lists
k12	Interest groups for teachers of kindergarten through grade 12
relcom	The Russian language interest group
sci	Science news and information
misc	An area for extraneous information and data
news	USENET issues and information
rec	Recreational activities (for example, fly fishing, golf, and biking)
soc	Sociology and psychology student interest topics
talk	USENET's talk or chat forum
u3b	AT&T 3B computer news
vmsnet	DEC VAX/VMS interest group

Protocols

Users can access your Internet server in a variety of ways. Your selection is determined by the hardware available to you for your server, the quantity and size of data to be made available to users, and how you want others to access your server.

The primary protocol used by Unix and Internet servers is commonly referred to only as TCP/IP, or Transmission Control Protocol/Internet Protocol. In actuality, TCP/IP consists of an entire suite of protocols, the most popular of which are listed below.

→ **IP (Internet Protocol).** This layer provides computer-to-computer transfer capabilities. IP is responsible for addressing and sending datagrams across an internet.

→ **TCP (Transmission Control Protocol).** This layer sits on top of the IP layer and provides a reliable connection-oriented channel between two connected computers. Error detection, flow control, and other connection services are located on the TCP layer.

→ **UDP (User Datagram Protocol).** This protocol is a simple, datagram-oriented, transport-layer protocol. Unlike TCP, it is not connection-oriented, and thus does not provide error checking or flow control.

→ **SLIP (Serial Line IP).** SLIP has for the most part become obsolete since the development of PPP. SLIP is a simple protocol used to transmit datagrams across a serial line.

→ **PPP (Point-to-Point Protocol).** This protocol has become the industry standard for transferring data across serial links. It has become more popular than SLIP because several protocols can be multiplexed across the serial link.

→ **ICMP (Internet Control Message Protocol).** ICMP handles error messages that are to be sent when datagrams are lost for whatever reason (for example, packet collisions).

Protocol Interface Nuances

Each protocol gives the attaching user a different look and variety of capabilities. An Internet server administrator must take into consideration the goal of the system and the technical abilities of those who are going to be accessing it. You, as an administrator, want to make your resources available to your intended audience in the most efficient manner possible. You must make it easy for others to access your data, which involves choosing the proper software protocol, hardware interface, security structure, and directory structure.

The Internet network was devised to be capable of managing data from multiple operating systems using various protocols. To date, FTP is still the most popular, but HTML (HyperText Markup Language)-based vehicles such as Gopher and World Wide Web are increasing in popularity. The following table shows the different kinds of Internet servers that are commonly used today with percentages indicating their popularity in use.

40%	File Transfer Protocol (FTP)
25%	Gopher & World Wide Web
20%	E-Mail Network News
6%	Remote Login (Telnet)
3%	Domain Name Lookup
6%	All other service (for example, WAIS)

FTP (File Transfer Protocol)

Some refer to FTP as a protocol; others refer to it as a program. Both are correct in that FTP (the program) uses FTP (the protocol) to copy files from one system to another. The majority of people connected to the Internet have access to FTP either directly through the command line or as a part of some Internet access program. Most Unix packages, as well as many Macintosh- and Intel-based TCP/IP client products, include the FTP program/protocol as standard.

Due to the popularity and availability of FTP, if you want easy access to your Internet server, consider this protocol. Furthermore, consider an FTP server setup; FTP enables you to store and distribute files for multiple operating system platforms.

Setup and Management

Your first consideration when implementing an FTP server is whether it is to be a secured FTP site or an anonymous one. Setting up your FTP presence first relies on your directory structure. You then can concern yourself with setting up your FTP server itself.

n o t e *Anonymous FTP* is, as the name suggests, a manner by which users (unknown to the server), can log in to a server and transfer files. You would log in to the system with your account being "anonymous" and your password as your account name (for example, matthew_arnett@lantimes.com).

If you want your system to be available to all users, designate it as an anonymous FTP server. In addition to enabling everyone access, many anonymous FTP sites further enable users to create personal subdirectories in which they can place personal files. This feature can be limited in any number of ways. Realize that as you allow anonymous users to create and store data, your hardware overhead increases.

Making an NT Internet server an anonymous FTP server is as simple as selecting the appropriate option during setup.

Most frequently, anonymous FTP sites are in place at companies that need to distribute programs or information to unknown customers. You can make available updated drivers for computer peripherals or post sales or product information immediately as it becomes available.

A secured server enables you to dictate who has access. Users first need to be granted access to your system, then access to your *full* system. This private system obviously offers much more security than that of the anonymous scenario; however, the administrator of a secure system must continually keep on top of who currently needs access to

what resources, which requires a great deal of time and is very easy to lose control of.

You can have the best of both worlds with your NT Internet server. You are not confined to having only a secure server or only an anonymous server. Your restrictions are only limited by your flexibility and ingenuity levels. You can create an anonymous user that needs to subscribe his or her real name and data. Until that user has done so, he or she can only access less sensitive information, such as your company portfolio or sales data. When a new user provides the proper information, you can allow various levels of access, depending on the user's needs (for example, personnel information or sales figures).

Resources can also be limited to certain users. Again, depending on an individual's needs, enable or disable that individual to create and maintain personal directories, files, or other assets.

Realize, however, that FTP is a file transfer protocol/program, and it is just that. You are limited in terms of the commands that you can perform, and thus you are limited in managing your system. Many third-party programs try to get around these limitations by adding and manipulating the FTP program unbeknownst to the user. This third-party bypass is fine, except that FTP is a standardized protocol with a very specific *request for comments* (RFC); no matter how the third-party software manufacturers manipulate the system, the base protocol is limited. They are restricted in what they can do while remaining truly FTP compliant. FTP was created to transfer files, and that's that.

Telnet

Telnet enables you to log in to a remote computer over a network (like the Internet) with TCP/IP. The utility literally enables you to log in to the remote system as if you were sitting at one of the terminals or workstations. The user accessing the remote computer executes a client program that connects to the server through a TCP connection. The remote workstation then takes and sends keystrokes to the server host as if its user were sitting directly on the system. Telnet is neither sophisticated nor flexible. It is, however, widely available and—like FTP—is used behind the scenes in many third-party access software.

Setup and Management

When you log in to a server that is set up with Telnet services, you only have access to areas your user account has access to. If you have multiple users who are going to log in to your system locally as well as remotely, you might want to consider implementing Telnet in a more widespread fashion. (If you need to set a user up, you might as well take advantage of the work you have already performed.)

rlogin

rlogin is a remote login program much like Telnet. rlogin, however, enables users on a WAN to remotely log in to multiple servers without having to present passwords each time they do so. Users can log in to multiple servers because the administrator sets user accounts up in a global environment with multiple machines.

The rlogin capabilities are mainly limited to Unix-based Internet servers. With Windows NT user and resource management, a strictly NT environment does not need rlogin. Because the Internet is still predominantly made up of Unix-based servers, however, you should at least know that rlogin exists and how it is used.

Setup and Management

rlogin is managed through the user setup on each of the different servers. The only difference is that access verification is transparent to the user, making it extremely simple for users to execute commands on remote servers, making it almost as easy as executing commands on the local server.

Gopher

Gopher was created at the University of Minnesota. It is one of the leading Internet tools in place today. The name Gopher was chosen for the University of Minnesota's school mascot.

Gopher services offer a simple way to navigate the Internet. The utility enables users to link to other Gopher servers through a user-friendly graphical user interface. Gopher service users move up and down directory structures just as they would navigate the Windows File Manager. Selecting subdirectories takes the user to another Gopher server or related subdirectory. Selecting a file automatically downloads the file.

Transversing a Gopher network (or *Gopherspace*) is seamless to the Gopher user. In addition to navigating Gopherspace in the aforementioned directory hierarchy manner, users can request information from an index server based on a search of user-supplied keywords.

Much of the Gopher access software enables users to view the information in a variety of formats. You can, for example, view data in English, German, or Spanish. You also can dictate whether the data is to be shown as a text file or as a Word for Windows document.

You can set your Gopher server up to make use of a local WAIS, or Wide Area Information Server, database.

Setup and Management

Microsoft strongly suggests that when setting up a Gopher server you use descriptive directory names, file names, and databases. Making them descriptive not only helps Gopher users navigate your system, but FTP users as well.

A hardware developer that wants to make available source code for a network interface card offers an example of a descriptive directory structure. The directory structure might look like \HARDWARE \NICS\MODELXYZ\BETA\VER11C.ASM. This example might allow beta users to obtain the latest version of a specific network interface card for testing. You could further create a descriptive alias for file VER11C.ASM, such as "Pre-release Beta code for NIC model XYZ." The Gopher client would see this description rather than the directory structure.

World Wide Web

The World Wide Web was developed at the European Laboratory for Particle Physics in Switzerland (or CERN). It has grown rapidly in popularity because of its multimedia capability over the Internet. The World Wide Web enables users to view graphics, to play video, and to listen to audio over the Internet.

If you want to make available data in the form of audio or video files, you want to use the World Wide Web. This inter-Internetwork is made up of WWW servers typically linked together by the Internet. The WWW provides information in hypertext format. This data is available in pages rather than the hierarchical directory structure of FTP and Gopher.

World Wide Web servers are linked together by hypertext entries. Being linked in this manner enables WWW users to transverse the WWW network by selecting a section of a WWW page. At the point of selection, the user is transported to the related directory and server. Each of these links are made possible through the use of a language called HyperText Markup Language (HTML). HTML, which is the standard WWW format, is made up of rather antique commands and symbols, similar to DOS.

Setup and Management

Until recently, you had to learn the HTML—with all its nuances—to create and maintain a World Wide Web server. This task is not only time consuming, but like any programming language, minor typing errors frequently result in drastic outcomes.

An increasing number of products are being created that help World Wide Web server administrators develop their Web pages. WebAuthor for Word for Windows by Quarterdeck Office Systems offers an example. WebAuthor uses WYSIWYG features to enable you to see exactly what you are creating, complete with embedded graphics and forms. This eliminates the need to repeatedly load the document in a browser to check its final form. Further, due to the fact that you are in Word for Windows, you can rearrange your layout as desired, as well as print the screen as it will appear to your end users.

Regardless of how you develop your HTML file, when a user accesses your WWW server, the WWW pages are sent as ASCII text files over the Internet. The receiving client receives the HTML file (which includes fonts and colors) and transforms them into the graphical user interface that the users observe.

In order to run a WWW server on your NT server, you need to install a HyperText Transfer Protocol (HTTP) Server Service. HTTP specifies the location of various resources by using Uniform Resource Locators (URLs) to publicize computers, directories, or files on the Internet.

t i p   The terms HTTP, World Wide Web, and Mosaic are frequently used interchangeably.

Electronic Mail

Setting up e-mail on the Internet is a very basic portion of establishing Internet connectivity. You need to set up electronic mailboxes for your users through either mailbots or mailing lists. Mailbots enable users to request information by sending a request to a mail robot's e-mail address. The alternative is to distribute information on an ongoing basis to a mail list.

Regardless of the specific reasons your company uses e-mail, it is the most popular transmission tool today. The reasons for using e-mail are vast and varied. A few of the more popular reasons follow:

→ E-mail eliminates missed telephone calls or data communications. It eliminates the need for everyone to be in the same time zone, or synchronized and ready to communicate at the same time.

→ You can reflect on and research your responses before returning correspondences.

→ The overall cost of transferring data is reduced as is the time that it takes to convey it.

WAIS

The Wide Area Information Server (WAIS) allows queries of index and distributed database queries. Both World Wide Web and Gopher servers make use of WAIS databases for their respective searches.

Setup and Management

With regard to the NT environment, you maintain the WAIS server service with the Services option in the NT Control Panel. Microsoft suggests that you periodically use Performance Monitor to ensure that your computer is not being too terribly taxed.

Hardware Interfaces

How are you going to physically attach to the Internet? ISDN? Ethernet? Dial-up? All of these options are viable depending on what you want to get out of having a presence on the Internet.

If you do not need to provide continuous Internet online accessibility, then dial-up is your least expensive option. As modems get faster and faster, however, prices become more and more reasonable. There is little excuse anymore to use a V.34/V.FC 28.8 kbps modem. Realize that to take advantage of the faster capabilities, your connection is only as fast as the slowest link.

Routers offer the second most reasonable solution for small- to medium-sized businesses. Internet access is provided by attaching to the Internet using a LAN IP account. Before you purchase the least expensive router to access the Internet, make sure that your service provider is compatible with the router you want to purchase. Many service providers also sell routers at a discounted price (if you use their service).

ISDN is growing in popularity faster than any other Internet access media, because telephone companies are replacing their older analog stepper or relay switches with modern digital units that can handle the higher data transferal speeds. Keep your eyes open for ISDN services in your area if they are not presently available.

Security Structures

The fact that a discussion of security falls this far into the chapter does in no way represent its level of importance (see Chapter 9, "Security and Configuration," for more information). We cannot stress enough the time and attention the issue of security warrants. You need to put in place at least some

form of deterrence against system hackers. Never underestimate the ability of others to do your system harm.

Plan for people to use your system in ways that you don't want (for example, they might send information along to others that is either corrupted or has some form of virus). As previously mentioned, your data is at stake as well as your company's integrity. Check files on a stand-alone system before you make them available for download.

Lastly, back up, back up, back up. Find a hardware/software combination that reliably backs up your system's lifeblood. Make sure that it also has a simplified restore procedure that you can perform without having to have a fully operational operating system. In most cases of a critical crash, you want to boot from a floppy and begin your restore procedure as soon as possible. The last thing you want is to have to install a full network operating system (NOS) before you can begin restoring the data. The NOS is already on the backup tapes, so why not be able to restore it all at once?

Software-only products, such as Cheyenne's Arcserve, can perform these actions.

Further, consider having data held on a separate software and hardware solution, such as IDAS's Highway Server. Take, for example, a company that manufactures modems. On the hardware side, you might have a directory structure similar to /DEVELOP/MODEM/PRODUCT0/HARDWARE/REV0000 and a software directory such as /DEVELOP/MODEM/PRODUCT0/SOFTWARE/REV0000.

Directory Structure

How you create and manage your directory structure determines how easy or difficult your system is to operate. Even though you might intend for all your users to use some form of graphical user interface for access (like World Wide Web or Gopher), you undoubtedly want to open your system to FTP users as well. Consequently, you will not always be able to rely on aliases or graphics to lead your users through the system.

You want to make your directory tree intuitive for command-line users to navigate without any extended assistance. For example, if your company develops hardware as well as software, you probably want to split the two early on in the tree for ease-of-use.

The issue of security offers another reason for taking care when developing your server directory tree. It is easier to start at the root directory with very few general permissions and increase user rights as you go further into the directory tree. If you keep the root of your directory tree very strictly regulated, then inherited rights are limited. You then have to assign rights as people need them (keeping security intact).

Projects to Which You Can Subscribe

Once you establish a presence on the Internet, you can join already established special-interest groups.

You can join special-interest groups usually by sending electronic mail to a group administrator in a structured format. Subsequently, whenever mail is set to the group, it is automatically forwarded to you as a group member.

Data Availability

All administrators of bulletin board systems and Internet servers are concerned with the integrity of the data on their system. Depending on the system type that you have chosen, you might want to consider creating one volume that is write-only for uploads. The creation of a write-only volume allows the Internet system administrator to view and test the files before others access and download them. Once the files have been verified as clean, they are placed in a directory (or on a separate volume), that is read-only and filescan allowed. These attributes allow users to search for, and download files to their local system.

part
· ·

System Administration

9

Security and Configuration

Now that you know how to get your server up and running on the Internet, you need to consider what you are going to do to manage the system, maximize performance, and control security. This is an ongoing task with Internet servers. As you find more files or services that you want to provide to clients, you must balance your resources against the services you want to provide.

And don't ever forget security. This is a major concern as you open your system up to literally millions of users around the world. You must take actions to protect your software and hardware. Don't wait until disaster strikes to take the security of your system seriously. You should have a security plan before you go online.

Management and security go together to give you the maximum usage of your new Windows NT Internet server.

Managing Your Windows NT Internet Server

With TCP/IP installed on your Windows NT machine, you now have some additional tools available to help you manage the system. These three tools are the SNMP Agent, Performance Monitor, and the Event Viewer. These three tools will help you get started with the task of optimizing your machine for peak efficiency.

Although these tools are not new with the installation of Internet Server software, you will notice several new monitoring options in the applications now available to you.

Using SNMP Management

The first thing you should do is to make sure that the Simple Network Management Protocol (SNMP) Service option is installed on your Windows NT server. This accomplishes two tasks:

note SNMP is a protocol used for network management data.

→ It installs the SNMP service, which allows your Windows NT computer to be administered remotely using remote SNMP management tools, like Sun NetManager or HP OpenView.

→ Installing this option also installs the appropriate tools so that you can monitor statistics for TCP/IP services with Performance Monitor. Windows NT's Performance Monitor will be discussed in more detail in the next section.

If you haven't already done so, follow these steps to install the SNMP Service option:

1. Double-click on the Networks icon in the Control Panel.

2. In the Network Settings dialog box, click on the Add **S**oftware button. In the Network Software Installation dialog box, choose TCP/IP Protocol and Related Components from the Add Software list.

3. When the TCP/IP Installation Options dialog box appears, select the **S**NMP Service option and click on OK. Windows NT copies the necessary files to your hard disk.

When you return to the Network Settings dialog box, select SNMP Service from the Installed Network Software list box. Click on the **C**onfigure button to bring up the SNMP Service Configuration dialog box (see fig. 9.1).

Figure 9.1

The SNMP Service Configuration dialog box.

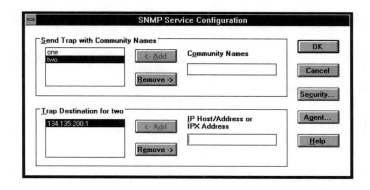

From this dialog box, you can configure the communities to which you want your computer to send traps, and the hosts for each community to which you send traps. Type the community name or host ID in the field on the right-hand side of the box; then click on the Add button.

 A trap is a block of data that indicates some request failed to authenticate. An SNMP service sends a trap when it receives a request for information with an incorrect community name.

If you are concerned about the security of your SNMP information, click on the Security button to open the SNMP Security Configuration dialog box (see fig. 9.2). You can configure three things about SNMP security from this box.

The Send Authentication Trap option sends a trap for failed authentications. If you want this option, select the Send Authentication Trap check box.

The Accepted Community Names option enables you to specify from which community names you accept requests. If the host is not on the list, the

SNMP service does not accept the request. To add community names to the list, insert the name into the field on the right; then click on the Add button.

The final SNMP security option enables you to specify from which hosts you accept SNMP packets. If you want to accept SNMP packets from any host, click on the Accept SNMP Packets from Any Host radio button. If you want to create a list of valid hosts, select Only Accept SNMP Packets from These Hosts. To add to the list, insert the host name or address in the field to the right; then click on Add.

When you finish configuring SNMP security, click on OK to return to the SNMP Service Configuration dialog box.

To configure the SNMP Agent, click on the Agent button. The SNMP Agent dialog box appears, giving you the option to enter some specific data about your machine (see fig. 9.3). You can insert a contact name and location in the appropriate fields.

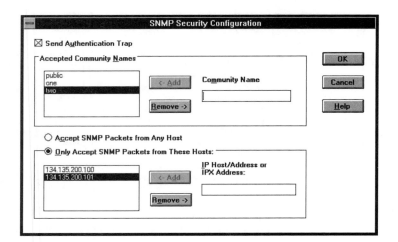

Figure 9.2

The SNMP Security Configuration dialog box.

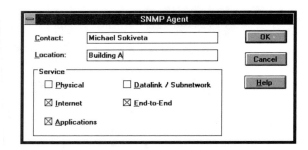

Figure 9.3

The SNMP Agent dialog box.

In the Service box, you can configure which services to report through SNMP. The services you select depend on the function of your Windows NT machine. Table 9.1 helps you to configure which services to report through SNMP.

When the agent is configured as you want, click on OK to return to the SNMP Service Configuration dialog box. Then click on OK again to close this box.

Using Performance Monitor

With TCP/IP components installed on your Windows NT computer, you now have a whole new batch of counters to watch from Performance Monitor.

 n o t e To use the TCP/IP performance counters, you should install the TCP/IP protocols and the SNMP Service.

Table 9.1

SNMP Agent Services

Option	Meaning
Physical	Select this option if your Windows NT computer manages any physical TCP/IP device, such as a repeater.
Datalink/Subnetwork	Select this option if your Windows NT computer manages a TCP/IP subnetwork or datalink, such as a bridge.
Internet	Select this option if your Windows NT computer acts as an IP gateway.
End-to-End	Select this option if your Windows NT computer acts as an IP host. This option should be selected for all Windows NT installations.
Applications	Select this option if your Windows NT computer includes any applications that use TCP/IP, such as e-mail. This option should be selected for all Windows NT installations.

With the SNMP Service installed, Performance Monitor provides additional objects to be monitored (see table 9.2).

 t i p If you are unsure what these objects and counters mean, click on the Explain button in the Add to Chart dialog box from within Performance Monitor, and you will see detailed explanations for each item.

All those statistics may be important to you at one time or another. Some you will want to monitor consistently, like the number of connections on your FTP server, or the number of files requested via FTP.

The information you gather here helps you realize when your server is becoming overloaded with process requests. If your machine is very busy as an FTP server, for example, you can move Gopher or HTTP server support to another Windows NT machine on the network.

Table 9.2 Manageable TCP/IP Objects and Their Counters

Object	Counters
IP	Datagrams Forwarded/sec
	Datagrams Outbound Discarded
	Datagrams Outbound No Route
	Datagrams Received Address Errors
	Datagrams Received Delivered/sec
	Datagrams Received Discarded
	Datagrams Received Header Errors
	Datagrams Received Unknown Protocol
	Datagrams Received/sec
	Datagrams Sent/sec
	Datagrams/sec
	Fragment Re-assembly Failures
	Fragmentation Failures
	Fragmented Datagrams/sec
	Fragments Created/sec
	Fragments Re-assembled/sec
	Fragments Received/sec
ICMP	Messages Outbound Errors
	Messages Received Errors
	Messages Received/sec
	Messages Sent/sec
	Messages/sec

Object	Counters
	Received Address Mask
	Received Address Mask Reply
	Received Destination Unreachable
	Received Echo Reply/sec
	Received Echo/sec
	Received Parameter Problem
	Received Redirect/sec
	Received Source Quench
	Received Time Exceeded
	Received Timestamp Reply/sec
	Received Timestamp/sec
	Sent Address Mask
	Sent Address Mask Reply
	Sent Destination Unreachable
	Sent Echo Reply/sec
	Sent Echo/sec
	Sent Parameter Problem
	Sent Redirect/sec
	Sent Source Quench
	Sent Time Exceeded
	Sent Timestamp Reply/sec
	Sent Timestamp/sec

continues

Table 9.2 Continued

Object	Counters
TCP	Connection Failures
	Connections Active
	Connections Established
	Connections Passive
	Connections Reset
	Segments Received/sec
	Segments Retransmitted/sec
	Segments Sent/sec
	Segments/sec
UDP	Datagrams No Port/sec
	Datagrams Received Errors
	Datagrams Received/sec
	Datagrams Sent/sec
	Datagrams/sec
FTP Server	Bytes Received/sec
	Bytes Sent/sec
	Bytes Total/sec
	Connection attempts
	Current Anonymous Users
	Current Connections
	Current Non-Anonymous Users
	Files Received

Object	Counters
	Files Sent
	Files Total
	Login Attempts
	Maximum Anonymous Users
	Maximum Connections
	Maximum Non-Anonymous Users
	Total Anonymous Users
	Total Non-Anonymous Users
WINS Server	Failed Queries/sec
	Failed Releases/sec
	Group Conflicts/sec
	Group Registrations/sec
	Group Renewals/sec
	Queries/sec
	Releases/sec
	Successful Queries/sec
	Successful Releases/sec
	Total Number of Conflicts/sec
	Total Number of Registrations/sec
	Total Number of Renewals/sec
	Unique Conflicts/sec
	Unique Registrations/sec
	Unique Renewals/sec

Using Event Viewer

Unfortunately, because the other server tools, like HTTP and Gopher, do not have hooks into the Performance Monitor utility, you need some other means to view them. As mentioned in Chapter 7, "Installing Server Applications," all the other server tools provided have their own means of creating transaction log files. Each one, by default, disables this feature, so you may want to enable transaction logging—especially in a new server.

Windows NT provides another tool that you shouldn't forget—the Event Viewer. Almost all system processes (including applications like Gopher and HTTP) record certain incidents to the Event Viewer. Check out your event log occasionally (more at first), and you can see system warnings, errors, or information messages. You can define filters so that you are viewing only those items that suit your needs. And you can save these filters for use whenever you want.

Use all the tools available to you, and you will have enough control over your system to provide the best services for your clients. If you don't keep on top of these things, you not only risk inefficiency, but something worse—a breach of security.

Securing Your Windows NT Internet Server

Security is always a concern to businesses that start providing services on the Internet. Unfortunately, many people in the world get great excitement out of sabotaging someone else's system just for kicks. But securing your system is about more than that.

As often as the intentional havoc is caused by hackers, unintentional havoc caused by some poor soul who doesn't know what he is doing is probably more common. Your goal is to protect against both kinds of users.

Deciding What to Protect

One of the first things you should decide is what you are trying to protect against. Are you worried about your files being deleted? Are you worried about someone planting a process that steals all your processing power or all your bandwidth? Are you worried about someone crashing your server? Or do you not care particularly about the server attached to the Internet, but about the other servers in your organization that are connected to it? Are you protected against natural disasters?

Each one of these problems requires a different strategy for confronting it. Know what your goals are, and you can implement the appropriate strategies.

Basic Security Measures

Before going any farther, it's important that you know and implement the basics for system security. These apply to any network server and should be starting points only.

Using a UPS

First, connect your server to an Uninterruptible Power Supply (UPS). It doesn't matter how many firewalls or passwords you set—if the power goes off, your unprotected server goes down. Windows

NT includes an applet in the Control Panel that provides you the means to keep your server running as long as possible, and then shut it down gracefully. Most UPSes are intelligent, meaning they can communicate with the server via a serial cable and provide the appropriate signals necessary for a graceful shutdown.

Backing Up Your System

Second, back up, back up, back up. No strategy for security and administration is complete without a backup plan. Back up your system's files at least once a day. Keep your tapes in rotation with some of them offsite. If your office is physically damaged, the tapes in your file cabinet aren't going to do you much good. Keep last week's tapes offsite somewhere in a secure place that you can get to easily in a crunch.

More and more third-party vendors are coming out with tape backup software for Windows NT systems. Look into some of those, or use the backup utility provided. There really is no excuse for not backing up your system. Do it regularly. There are only two kinds of servers: those that have crashed and those that will. Be ready, and you will save yourself many headaches later on.

Protecting with NTFS

Next, use the NT File System (NTFS) available with Windows NT. The FAT file system doesn't provide any security—anyone can take a simple boot disk and access your files at will. If you want a FAT partition on your disk, fine. But create an NTFS partition as well and install Windows NT and other

server files to that partition. Then use the security options when you share a resource to the outside world.

Put your FTP server files on their own NTFS partition and make sure that users have read-only access. Put your FTP upload area (if you decide to have one) on a separate partition and grant write-only rights to it. Do the same for your other server applications. Check the security settings of your resources periodically to make sure that they match your intentions.

User Account Specifications

Finally, enforce user security. When you set up a user account on your Windows NT system, you have the option of controlling some of the password settings. Don't just ignore this tool, use it (see fig. 9.4). Make sure that your users update their passwords regularly by setting a maximum password age. Don't permit blank passwords. Make sure that the passwords are difficult to guess by setting a minimum password length. Have Windows NT make sure that unique passwords are used often by keeping a password history.

Control the accounts by allowing only so many bad login attempts before the account is disabled. Enforce login times, and kick users out (gracefully!) when the logon hours expire.

Enable the auditing policies of your system (see fig. 9.5). Keep track of who tries to change what parameters. By default, auditing is turned off; but this is not recommended under any circumstances.

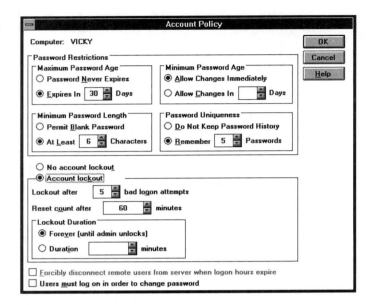

Figure 9.4

Configuring account policies.

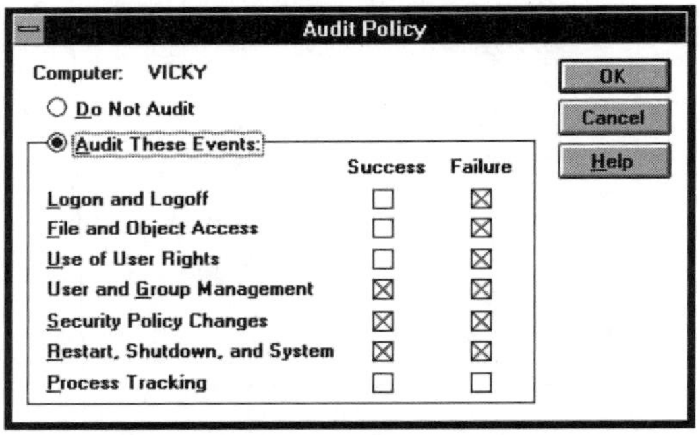

Figure 9.5

Configuring your system's audit policy.

Only grant users the rights they need. Don't give everyone the Administrator equivalence just because it's easy. It takes a little time to set up, but it will undoubtedly save you in the long run.

If users give you hassles because of the limitations, remind them that you are on the Internet now. The relaxed security policies of the past no longer apply. If your company is to stay in business, security has to be a priority.

More Security Measures

You will also want to protect your system with some sort of disk redundancy. Use the Disk Administrator utility in the Administrative Tools group to mirror or stripe a number of disks. That way, in case one disk fails, your system will stay up and running until you can replace the faulty hard drive. To mirror or stripe your disks, select `Disk Volumes` on the screen, then choose the Mirror and Striping option from the menu.

Also, beware of viruses. Connecting your system to the Internet means that you open yourself up to all sorts of problems, including viruses. If you have an upload area on your FTP server, make sure that you scan any files that come in for viruses. And scan your whole system at least once a day. If you find an infected file, you have a backup to restore from.

Physical Security

How you connect your Windows NT server to the Internet is probably the most important part of security. You can choose from five different models to follow when deciding how to make your Internet connection. This chapters starts with the most secure, and then works down to the least secure.

Physical Isolation

The most secure way to provide Internet services is with the *Physical Isolation model* (see fig. 9.6).

In this model, the server is completely isolated from the rest of your network. This is not only the most secure way to connect to the Internet, but the easiest to plan and configure. Two-way IP communication exists between your server and the Internet, but no traffic passes to your production LAN. If your system is damaged, then you rebuild it with backups.

Figure 9.6

The Physical Isolation model.

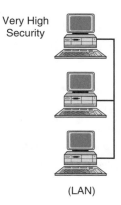

Very High Security

(LAN)

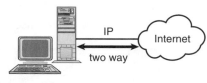

Physical Isolation

IP

two way

Internet

(Internet Server)

The biggest drawback to this model is that you cannot share files between the corporate network and the Internet. Clients cannot get out to the Internet directly; they must go to the server to do so.

You can expand this model and connect a small LAN to the server. This LAN is on a completely different physical segment from your production LAN. Client computers, called *kiosks*, that are part of this LAN can be placed in common locations throughout your office like conference or break rooms. Just make sure that the LAN segment stays physically separated from your corporate network.

Protocol Isolation

The *Protocol Isolation model* offers slightly less security but has a few more usability advantages (see fig. 9.7).

This model gives network clients access to the Internet server through a different protocol from the protocol of the Internet. It involves installing two network adapters in your Windows NT Internet server. One adapter is bound to the IP protocol and is connected to the Internet. The other adapter is bound to the IPX protocol and uses this protocol to communicate with other network clients.

It is very useful if you want to be able to place files on your server for Internet clients to access—resources are accessible from either direction. However, the LAN clients cannot directly access the Internet.

Keep in mind that, theoretically, a hacker could penetrate this security model, but it would be very difficult because the server does not perform protocol conversion or routing.

This model has a variation also. You can place an additional server between the LAN clients and the Internet server and configure Windows NT to replicate the files between the two servers. This gives you more control over what is brought into the LAN and is permitted outside the LAN. Additionally, files can be checked for viruses before they are replicated to the LAN server.

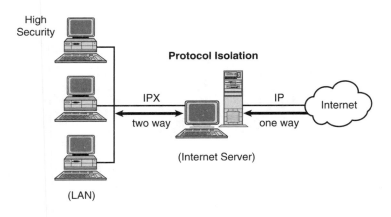

Figure 9.7

The Protocol Isolation model.

Third-Party Router Model

The third model, which portrays third-party routers, requires additional hardware and software from a third-party vendor, but provides a high level of security (see fig. 9.8).

If you are using a large corporate network with several subnets, you will probably want to implement the *Third-Party Router model*. This is usually used in conjunction with a leased line to the Internet. Many third-party routers can be used as firewalls creating a somewhat secure environment by filtering out unwanted packets. Depending on the security capabilities of your router, this model can offer a high level of security.

Windows NT Router Isolation Model

The fourth model to review is the *Windows NT Router Isolation model*. This model involves setting up two TCP/IP adapters in your Internet server,

but disabling the Internet routing features of Windows NT (see fig. 9.9).

This type of model offers good security because, in a sense, you are using your Windows NT server as a firewall. The biggest problem with this model is that your whole security strategy depends on whether a little check box is cleared in the TCP/IP configuration dialog box. This, of course, corresponds to an entry in your Registry database; and if anyone were to hack their way into the Registry and change that value, you would have no security.

Full Access Model

The last model to discuss is the *Full Access model*. As you can probably determine by the name, this model offers very little security. In fact, you are dependent on the security system of the file system and the applications to keep any unwanted users out (see fig. 9.10).

Figure 9.8

The Third-Party Router model.

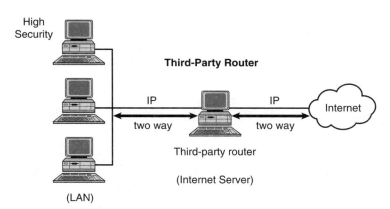

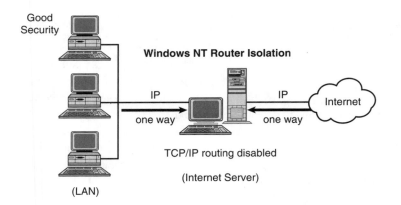

Figure 9.9

The Windows NT Router Isolation model.

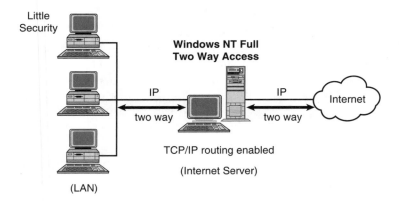

Figure 9.10

The Full Access model.

This is the same physical setup as the previous model but with TCP/IP routing enabled. The LAN clients have unrestricted use of the Internet gateway, and Internet users have full access to your LAN. If security is a consideration at all, you shouldn't implement this model.

Keep in mind that Windows NT is not well suited as a TCP/IP router. It does not process Router Information Protocol (RIP) requests that automatically maintain a TCP/IP router's table. Without the table, the overhead can be quite large.

Summary

When your Windows NT server is up and running, the battle is only half over. Now you can begin the task of administering your server and making sure that the data remain intact. Windows NT provides several tools to help you in this quest. The SNMP Services, the Performance Monitor, and the Event Viewer can be a great help in keeping you informed of what's going on at the server level.

As for security, use the tools provided with Windows NT to keep your system safe and secure. These utilities include audit logs, user account options, backup capabilities, UPS tools, etc. Plan your Internet connection with security in mind. If security is very important, don't forget to check out the third-party options available to you in the form of routers and firewalls.

10

Planning for the Internet Server

By now you have learned all the steps you need to take in order to set up your Windows NT server for use on the Internet. This chapter takes you through those steps and helps you make decisions concerning what services to provide, how to configure your system for security, and how to ensure that your server is ready to provide services to Internet clients.

Identifying Your Objectives

At this point, you probably have a good handle on the capabilities of an Internet Server. If not, reread Chapter 7, "Installing Server Applications." You now must make some decisions about the kind of services you want to provide to users on the Internet. Before you get started, make sure you have read Chapter 8, "Maintaining the Internet Server." This chapter explains some of the things you can do with each type of server.

FTP Server

If you simply want to provide files to clients on the Internet, then you probably want to set up an FTP server. Many software companies provide updated drivers, patches, and support files on their FTP servers; but even if your company doesn't write software, you still can provide files for others to download.

Some companies, for example, scan pictures of their products, save them to files, and place those picture files on an FTP server. You can put on the server press releases announcing new products your company is developing or changes in your organization. Company backgrounds and executive biographies can be placed on the server as well.

If your company publishes a newsletter, that newsletter can be placed on an FTP server. If your business is publishing, you can put back issues of articles or entire magazines on your server for clients to download.

Perhaps your server is not associated with a company. Maybe you are building a server strictly for fans of your favorite music star. Many servers on the Internet exist for this purpose, providing the latest concert information, lyric sheets, and little known facts pertaining to celebrities. The Internet can be a great way for fans to communicate and share information.

An FTP server provides the same for hobbyists. If working with model railroads is your thing, you can reserve an area on your FTP server that has layouts of the best tracks. Create an FTP server for your mountain-biking friends to share descriptions of the hottest places to ride with instructions on how to get there and what they need to bring.

Almost every hobby and fan club in existence already has much of this information somewhere on an FTP server, but if you think you can do it better, go right ahead.

Transferring files is one of the first uses of the Internet, and it remains the most popular use today.

HTTP Server

If you want to get a little more flashy in your presentation to Internet clients, consider setting up an HTTP, or HyperText Transfer Protocol, server. The HTTP server, which is also often called a Web server, gives you the flexibility to add graphics, sound, or video to the presentation to clients. It also enables you to link information on a global scale.

One of the best parts of "surfing the Net" is checking out the interesting and colorful Web pages different organizations have created. The first screen users see when they access your WWW server with a browser is called the *home page*. The home page usually provides links to other screens or services. In addition to your home page, for example, one of the first links usually set up on a server is to a "What's New" section. Guide users through your latest products, your best deals, or your finest stuff, and you get a chance to make an impression.

You don't have to be selling a product or service to benefit from setting up a Web site. Many organizations and individuals have created home pages that deal only with their personal interests or hobbies. A Web page exists for almost everything imaginable.

There are Web sites for the White House, universities, government agencies, and Slovian wine shops. On one hand, it's nice to have the freedom to put whatever you want on your Web page, but on the other hand, realize what you're competing with at the user's end. Consequently, you should work hard to make your home page as interesting as possible.

 This brings up a point worth considering. Setting up an HTTP server requires working in the *Hyper Text Markup Language* (HTML). HTML tells the Web browser (the most common browser is Mosaic) how to lay out the text and how to make links to other parts or documents. Making a Web home page can be tedious work. Learning how to create an HTML document is still very difficult, but new tools are coming out every day that make the job easier.

HTML programming, however, will always be somewhat of an art form. You're often dealing with pictures, and the more interesting things you display on-screen, the more people you'll have wanting to visit your site.

If setting up an HTTP server is something you want to try, install the software as directed in Chapter 7. Web servers have become the most popular (and interesting) servers on the Internet. As the saying goes, "If you build it, they will come."

Gopher Server

Because so much information is available on the Internet, it is very easy to be overwhelmed. It's hard to know where to look for the information you want, and there is far too much to sift through. While FTP and Telnet are the most popular means for getting information from other systems, if you don't know exactly what you are looking for and precisely where it is, you will have a hard time finding it.

In order to combat this feeling of being overwhelmed, and to facilitate the search process for people, Gopher was developed. The server provides an index of information on the Internet. One Gopher server, of course, cannot keep up with all the data the Internet holds, but it does not have to. Gopher servers often are interconnected and cross-referenced so that one Gopher server has information and links to other Gopher servers with their information and links, and so on.

With Gopher client software, users do not have to know exactly where certain data or files exist before they go searching. All a user needs to know is the address of a Gopher server; that server presents the information in a clear, structured, hierarchical list. The complexity or simplicity of the information matters not.

If you would like to set up a Gopher server, follow the directions in Chapter 7. If you are worried about users being able to find your server and figuring out all the services you provide, setting up a Gopher server can help clients as they explore the Internet.

WAIS Server

Like Gopher, the *Wide Area Information Server* or (WAIS—pronounced "ways"), uses the client-server model to navigate around data resources. A WAIS client talks to a WAIS server and asks it to perform a search for data containing a specific word or series of words.

WAIS is based on the Z39.50 standard. Z39.50 is similar to the *Structure Query Language* (SQL), but it is more simple and general. The WAIS Server for

Windows NT included with this book implements a subset of the Z39.50-88 protocol, with WAIS-specific extensions.

You also want to install the set of tools used to prepare and search full-text databases for computers running the Windows NT operating system. This set of tools is important if you plan to use the searching capabilities of the Gopher server, the HTTP server, or the WAIS server.

Flowchart (Decision Tree)

Figure 10.1 depicts the types of servers that you can build with Windows NT Server based on your specific needs. Use and refer to this flow chart throughout the decision-making process of building a Windows NT Internet server.

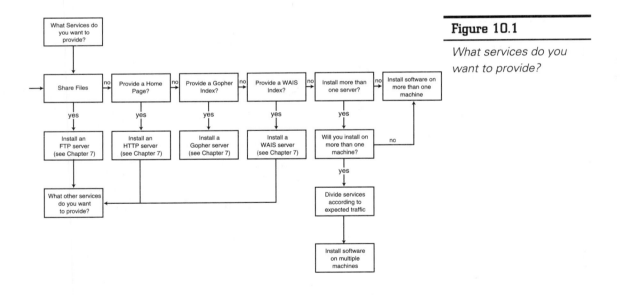

Figure 10.1

What services do you want to provide?

Planning for Security

Before getting too far into the planning of your Internet server, be sure to consider the security issues. Your security strategy basically has three parts.

The first part has to do with using network protocols and topology to provide security. Chapter 9, "Security and Configuration," discusses five different ways to connect your network server to the Internet. Some models provide high security; some provide very little. You must decide which model to follow in designing your security strategy.

The second part of your security tactics should include the design of the server itself. Pay attention to the way you partition your file system. Put the files you intend to share through FTP in one read-only partition, for example, and on another write-only partition, create a place where users can place their files. Simple organization takes advantage of the security capabilities of Windows NT.

Finally, don't forget the basic practices of security in any computer environment. Back up your system regularly, scan often for computer viruses, and enable the auditing and alert capabilities. Not everyone on the Internet is trying to sabotage your server, but those who sabotage aren't your only worry. Setting up a secure system protects against even the more innocent users who inadvertently put files where they don't belong or delete files that need to be there.

The only completely secure system, of course, is the one never turned on. That won't do you much good though. You have to balance your security needs with the services you are trying to provide (see fig. 10.2).

Figure 10.2

Design your security strategy.

Security Checklist

✔ Choose a topology to match your security needs
✔ Partition your server (use NTFS)
✔ Plug in a UPS
✔ Design and implement a regular backup strategy
✔ Install virus scanner(s)
✔ Enable error and information logs
✔ Enable auditing
✔ Configure user authentication security
✔ Install a firewall
✔ Implement hardware redundancy
✔ Physically isolate your server from other users

Estimating Traffic Flow

The next decision you must make about connecting your Windows NT server to the Internet is the type of connection you want to provide. Here you really need to balance performance needs and cost. If you have never set up an Internet server for your company, it can be hard to predict the type of traffic you'll see. You certainly don't want to pay for a high speed link if you only see three clients a day accessing your server.

Generally, bandwidth price is directly proportional to its size—a 384 Kbps link, for example, costs more than a 56 Kbps link. Selecting the right amount of bandwidth and the right type of WAN access service is critical. For help on determining your bandwidth requirements, see Chapter 4, "Internet Access Services." Realistically assess your bandwidth needs, evaluate different services in relation to your needs, and then select an *Internet Access Provider* (IAP) that offers the best type of WAN bandwidth service. You have several options:

- Analog dial-up services (not too practical for a full-time server)
- Switched digital services, including ISDN and Switched 56
- Dedicated WAN services, including Frame Relay and Point-to-Point Leased (or Dedicated) lines

Dial-Up Options

As the name indicates, dial-up services are not always "on," whereas dedicated services are up 24 hours a day, whether someone is using them or not. In dial-up, you pay for what you use (the amount of time the connection is up)—the connection times are metered. With dedicated connections, however, you essentially "lease" the line and pay a fee that is independent of the usage level. Your dial-up service can be used in a dedicated line mode, however, if the connection is kept open all the time to a preset location. This option is very common for Internet access in cases where only a local unmetered call is needed from your house or office to the nearest IAP.

From an IAP's standpoint, if the IAP does not have to assign a static IP address and dedicate a port and a modem specifically for the customer, you have a dial-up service. The IAP does not wake up your host for a dial-up connection. In other words, it won't call your computer if someone on the Internet wants to access your host when you are not connected to the Internet.

Switched Digital Options

Switched digital services have become popular in the last few years. The most commonly available switched digital service in the U.S. is Switched 56 Kbps. ISDN, however, is quickly becoming the universal standard for switched digital access in today's environment. ISDN is now readily available in most metropolitan areas within the U.S. and in most industrial countries, such as Japan, Germany, the U.K., and France.

Dedicated WAN Services

One of the newest technologies to emerge in the last few years in the area of wide area networking is called *Frame Relay*. Frame Relay is a packet-switching protocol with speed ranges from 56 Kbps to 45 Mbps. Frame Relay delivers a low-delay, high-throughput connection. Frame Relay relies on availability of superior quality lines, such as fiber, that are common in today's telephone networks. Frame Relay expects clear, high-quality lines to guarantee virtually error-free transmissions. If errors do occur, it is the responsibility of intelligent end devices to request retransmission.

One of the major benefits Frame Relay offers is that the price is distance-insensitive—the distance the call travels does not affect the hourly rate for the call. That is why Frame Relay is being used extensively in the wide area networking environments of different companies. If Frame Relay is already a standard for your wide area communications, use it to connect to the Internet. Frame Relay standards already guarantee interpretability with the Internet protocol, and are set by the Frame Relay Forum.

Previously, the T1 trunk was the high-end option for Point-to-Point Dedicated lines, and is the one that is still most frequently used. A T1 trunk supports transfer speeds up to 1.544 megabits per second. In Europe, E1 is the equivalent service, offering bandwidth of up to 2.048 Mbps. For companies that don't require this much throughput, telephone companies have begun offering *Fractional T1* (FT1) services. FT1 services are configured as a number of 56 Kbps channels. In spite of the popularity of the T1 service, the emerging high-end option for a Point-to-Point Dedicated connection is the T3 line, which supports a 45 Mbps connection. Today, very few sites in the country require a T3 line as their Internet connection, which will most likely continue to be the case for the immediate future. Not until you start using much higher bandwidth applications, or start to use the Internet as a wide area backbone, is this case likely to change.

For definitions of the terms used in the above paragraph, refer to Chapter 4.

Frame Relay and Point-to-Point Dedicated lines are both recommended services if you need to support both inbound and outbound Internet connections, or if you intend to host your own Web server. If you are using Frame Relay for 56 Kbps connections, your actual bandwidth is identical to a Switched 56 Kbps or ISDN connection.

The actual throughput your applications see does not vary significantly between Frame Relay and Point-to-Point Dedicated lines. The primary economic benefit of Frame Relay—distance-insensitive pricing—is inconsequential when connecting to the Internet because most companies can find an Internet access provider relatively nearby. For this reason, Point-to-Point Dedicated lines are a popular alternative for companies requiring a high-speed, permanent Internet connection. Figure 10.3 illustrates the two types of connections.

	Analog	ISDN	Switched 56 Kbps	Frame Relay	Point-to-Point Dedicated
Bandwidth	14.4 or 28.8 Kbps	56/64 or 112/128 Kbps	56 Kbps	56 Kbps to 1.5 Mbps	56 Kbps to 1.5 Mbps
Call Setup Time	30 seconds and up	Less than 5 seconds	Less than 20 seconds	Negligible	None
Tariff Structure	Fixed or Per Minute	Fixed or Per Minute	Fixed or Per Minute	Fixed	Fixed
Availability	High	Medium	High	Medium	High
Suitable for Inbound Access	Only if line is kept on all the time	Only if line is kept on all the time	Only if line is kept on all the time	Yes	Yes

Figure 10.3

Decide the type of connection you want to implement.

Testing and Verifying

One last step you need to consider before connecting your server to the Internet involves testing your machine as a server in a lab environment. This testing serves a few purposes. First, you get to make sure that everything is installed properly and that the software is going to perform as you intended. Second, it allows you to verify the security system you set up. And third, you can confirm your choices for supplemental tools, such as backup and anti-virus software.

Checking Installation of Software

Use client tools—such as the ones described in Appendix B, "Guide to Client Applications"—to make sure the server software you installed is configured properly. It's one thing to check the software yourself and verify that it really works the way you want it to, and another to have an irate user call your office because he or she cannot get to the files promised on your Web server.

Make sure the error and audit logs are performing properly and that they are giving you the information you need. You have created a new system, and that system needs to be examined before it goes online, just like any other server on your network. With this system, however, you're opening up to the world.

Verifying the Security

Verifying the security of your Internet server can be tricky because so much needs to be considered. Make sure you check the obvious, such as whether or not a user can delete files to which he or she should have read-only rights. Look for security holes, and try to do the types of actions you know a user should not be able to do. An Internet server is a complicated system, making it very easy to overlook something.

If security is critical, hire a security specialist to try to break in to your system before you put it online. These consultants use special tools that test a system for weaknesses. Your goal is for the consultant to find those weaknesses before anyone else does.

Validating Your Tools

Hopefully, you have other tools on your system helping to maintain its integrity. Check these tools often to make sure they are working. Back up your system and restore it to another machine so you know what that process involves before you get in a crunch. Test the integrity of the information that was backed up to make sure it matches the original data. Verify that the user accounts are still intact with the same configuration.

Is your archive package backing up only files, or does it back up user account information? Is it backing up all the partitions, or does it default to just the one the system is on? You don't want to be surprised with these answers when you're scrambling to get a server online. Is your backup hardware plugged into the *Uninterruptable Power Supply* (UPS) so that it will continue to run when the power fails?

Make sure your anti-virus software is running constantly (if that is your plan). Ideally, configure your system so that the software starts when the system boots, so you don't have to start the software manually (you might forget). Also, perform scans regularly—if possible, once a day. Matched with a daily backup strategy, the most you will lose is a day's worth of effort.

Test your UPS and the accompanying software. Does it really shut down your system in an orderly fashion? Does the "advertised" battery life match the life you see with all your server's peripherals plugged in?

This is only a partial list—try anything else you can think of to test your system. You want to minimize the surprises when you set up your Windows NT Internet server. The old saying, "An ounce of prevention is worth a pound of cure," applies here.

Summary

This chapter provides an overview of the information you need to set up a Windows NT Internet server. You need to decide what you are trying to accomplish, what risks you are willing to take in defining your security strategy, and what the best connectivity options are. Then, before you connect to the world, test like crazy. It's better for *you* to break your system than for an Internet client to, intentionally or not. And if something does happen, you will be ready.

The Internet provides a unique marketplace for you to promote your wares. It can be a tool of research, fun, discovery, and solutions. By connecting your server to the Internet, you are taking part in an information revolution. Information brings knowledge; knowledge brings potential power.

part

• •

Appendixes

Internet Service Providers

Version 1.4   April 19, 1994

Purpose

Hopefully, this document will help the reader find an e-mail or Internet Network solution that is suitable to the reader's requirements. All providers have services for users and organizations to connect to the Internet.

Home Site

This document can always be found on the Internet Society's information servers. The current URL is:

gopher://isoc.and.ietf/faq/ Network_Service_Providers_Around_the_World

Format

This document lists information in the following format:

E-mail/Network Service Provider:
Postal Address:
TEL:
FAX:
E-mail:

Area Served:

Services:

Last Updated:

The Area Served entry states the geographic region or specific community the provider serves (for example, Academic, Research & Development, Commercial, Public Access, Professional Societies, User Groups, and so on).

The Services entry can include any of the following:

→ **Terminal.** Terminal access (also called dial-up host) enables users to connect through a modem and terminal emulation software to a system providing services. This usually means a Unix shell account. The services these systems usually provide inlcude e-mail, FTP, Telnet, and USEnet News. Other services might include Gopher, WWW, IRC, and other Internet services. Check with the provider for details.

→ **Personal Information Services.** Personal Information Services provides a comprehensive suite of news entertainment, travel planning, conferencing, communications, and many other services. All can be accessed through a terminal emulator. Most provide a client to load on the PC or MAC.

→ **Network Connections.** These providers offer a full range of dial-up and dedicated network links to regional, national, and international networks.

 Most providers who offer network connects, also offer e-mail, SLIP, PPP, and UUCP solutions.

→ **Personal IP.** The provider offers SLIP, PPP, and ISDN connections. The SLIP/PPP/ISDN links can be used for a personal workstation or a small LAN. This service enables an individual to have direct access to the Internet. Their personal workstation becomes a node on the Internet through a dial-up SLIP, PPP, or ISDN connections.

→ **Client/Server.** The provider supplies a PC or MAC client that interfaces with their services. The client helps the user manage the services they use most and saves money on connect charges. The client enables the user to prepare the information to be sent (such as e-mail messages, fax messages, and so on), connect to the server, upload prepared material, and download anything waiting for the users. The users can then read downloaded information at their leisure.

→ **UUCP.** Many providers offer UUCP e-mail and USEnet News service. This enables sites to dial-in and transfer e-mail and news. Some providers offer an option to poll the site, and pick and deliver e-mail and news in the queue.

→ **Wireless.** Wireless network connections offer a user access to the provider through a wireless modem. Some services include e-mail, USEnet News, and batch file transfer.

→ **Business Services.** The provider offers a wide variety of business communications services for users at home, work, or traveling.

→ **Special.** These are unique services that only one or two providers offer.

→ **X.400.** The provider is an X.400 Administrative Management Domain (ADMD) who provides e-mail services.

Other Sources

The information in this document is gained directly from the service provider. Queries are periodically sent to each service provider to ensure the accuracy of the information. In addition to this document, other sources can be used to find an e-mail/Network service provider, including the following:

1. SRI International. File: Internet-access-providers-alphabetical-listing.txt on anonymous FTP host: ftp.nisc.sri.com (Sept. 28, 1992).

2. CONCISE Archive. Anonymous FTP at concise.level-7.co.uk.

3. International Telecommunications Union (ITU) Gopher. (info.itu.ch) This site hosts a comprehensive list of X.400 service providers around the world.

4. INTERNIC Gopher. is.internic.net.

5. Low Cost Networking Resource Center Gopher. rain.psg.com.

6. The Public Dialup Internet Access List (PDIAL). File: PDIAL010.TXT by Peter Kaminski. To get the PDIAL, send e-mail with the subject "Send PDIAL" to "info-deli-server@netcom.com."

7. The Forgotten Sites List by Louis Raphael. This list is available by anonymous FTP from freedom.nmsu.edu in /pub/docs/fslist. The name of the file is "fslist-X" where X is the version number. It also is available from login.qc.ca in /pub/fslist/FSLIST-X where X is the version number.

8. DLIST. A list of dedicated line Internet providers by Susan Estrada. Send e-mail to dlist@ora.com.

9. Network Sevice Providers in Latin America and Caribe. Copies can be picked up on the Peru Internet Network, Red Cientifica Peruana Gopher: URL:gopher://gopher.rcp.net.pe:70/ or e-mailed from Yuri Herrera at: odi@rcp.net.pe.

10. Connectivity with Africa by Randy Bush (randy@psg.com). You can get the current version of the file at any time from the following two primary means:

URL:gopher://gopher.psg.com:70/0/0/networks/connect/africa.txt

or by sending e-mail to the automatic server:

To: server@gopher.psg.com
From: <your address>
Subject: send pub/gopher-data/networks/connect/africa.txt

Updates

Please send any additions, changes, or deletions to Barry Raveendran Greene at:

greenebr@aplcomm.jhuapl.edu

Service Providers Listing

AARNet (The Australian Academic and Research Network)
GPO Box 1142
Canberra ACT 2601
AUSTRALIA
TEL: +61 6 249 3385
E-mail: G.Huston@aarnet.edu.au
Area Served: Australia

a2i communications
1211 Park Avenue #202
San Jose, CA 95126-2924
E-mail: info@rahul.net
Area Served: San Jose, CA, area (408 area code)
Services: Terminal

ACM Network Services
PO BOX 21599
Waco, TX 76702
TEL: (817) 776-6876
FAX: (817) 751-7785
E-mail: Account-Info@ACM.org
Area Served: world
Services: Terminal, UUCP
Last Update: 3/17/94

ACONET
Austrian Scientific Data Network
ACONET-Verein
Gusshausstrasse 25
A-1040 Wien
AUSTRIA
Attn: Florian Schnabel
TEL: +43 1 436111 or +43 222 58801 3605
E-mail: helpdesk@aco.net
schnabel@edvz.tu-graz.ada.at
schnabel@fstgss01.tu-graz.ac.at
C=at; ADMD=ada; PRMD=aconet; O=wep; S=helpdesk
C=at; ADMD=ada; PRMD=tu-graz; O=edvz; S=schnabel
Area Served: Austria

Actrix Information Exchange
P.O. Box 11-410
Wellington NEW ZEALAND
TEL: +64 4 499-1708
FAX: +64 4 389-6356
E-mail: john@actrix.gen.nz
Area Served: New Zealand
Services: Terminal
Last Update: 2/23/94

AlterNet

3110 Fairview Park Drive
Suite 570
Falls Church, VA 22042
USA
TEL: +1 800 488 6384 or +1 703 204 8000
FAX: +1 703 204 8001
E-mail: alternet-info@uunet.uu.net
Area Served: U.S.
Services: Network Connections

Alternex

IBASE
Rua Vicente de Souza 29
22251 Rio de Janiero
BRAZIL
TEL: +55 (21) 286 0348
FAX: +55 (21) 286 0541
E-mail: suporte@ax.apc.org
Area Served: Brazil
Services: Terminal, UUCP

America Online, Inc.

8619 Westwood Center Drive
Vienna, VA 22182-2285
USA
TEL: 1-800 827 6364   or   +1 703 8933 6288
E-mail: info@aol.com
Area Served: U.S. and Canada
Services: Personal Information Service, Client/
Server

AMT Solutions Group Inc. - Island Net

P.O. Box 6201 Depot 1
Victoria B.C.
V8P 5L5
CANADA

TEL: (604) 727-6030
FAX: (604) 478-7343
E-mail: mark@amtsgi.bc.ca
Area Served: Victoria and area, British Columbia
Services: Terminal
Last Update: 1/28/94

Anomaly

Anomaly—Rhode Island's Gateway To The Internet
TEL: +1 401 273 4669
E-mail: info@anomaly.sbs.risc.net
Area Served: Providence RI (area codes 401, 508)
Services: Terminal

ANS

(Advanced Network and Services, Inc.)
2901 Hubbard Rd.
Ann Arbor, MI 48105
USA
TEL: 800 456 8267 or   +1 313 663 2482
E-mail: info@ans.net
Area Served: U.S. and International
Services: Network Connections

ANTENNA

Box 1513
NL-6501 BM Nijmegen
Netherlands
TEL: +31(80)235372
FAX: +31(80)236798
E-mail: support@antenna.nl
Area Served: Netherlands
Services: Terminal, UUCP

Anterior Technology

P.O. Box 1206
Menlo Park, CA 94026-1206

USA
TEL: +1 415 328 5615
FAX: +1 415 322 1753
E-mail: info@radiomail.net
Area Served: San Francisco Bay area
Services: Terminal; UUCP; Wireless: E-mail.

APK, Public Access UNI*
19709 Mohican Ave.
Cleveland, OH 44119
TEL: data - 216-481-9436
216-481-1960
VOICE: 216-481-9428
FAX: 216-481-9428x33
E-mail: zbig@wariat.org
Area Served: Cleveland Ohio (216 area code)
Services: Terminal, UUCP
Last Update: 3/17/94

ARIADNE
NRC DEMOKRITOS
153 10 Attiki-Athens
Greece
TEL: +30 1 6513392   or   +30 1 6536351
FAX: +30 1 6532910   o   +30 1 6532175
E-mail: postmaster@isosun.ariadne-t.gr
postmast@grathdem (Bitnet)
S=postmaster; OU=isosun; O=ariadne-t;
P=ariadne-t;C=gr;
Area Served: Greece

ARNES
ARNES Network
Jamova 39, Ljubljana
SLOVENIA
Attn: Marko Bonac
TEL: +38 61 159199
FAX: +38 61 161 029

E-mail: helpdesk@ijs.si
C=si; ADMD=mail; PRMD=ac; O=ijs; S=helpdesk
Area Served: Slovenia

ARnet (Alberta Research Network)
Director of Information Systems
Alberta Research Council
Box 8330, Station F
Edmonton, Alberta
CANADA, T6H 5X2
Attn: RALPH PENNOTEL: +1 403 450 5188
FAX: +1 403 461 2651
E-mail: arnet@arc.ab.ca
penno@arc.ab.ca
Area Served: Alberta, Canada
Services: Network Connections
Last Updated: 5 Jan 1994

ARNET (Argentine Science Network)
UNDP Project ARG-86-026
Ministerio de Relaciones Exteriores y Culto
Reconquista 1088 1er. Piso - Informatica
(1003) Capital Federal
Buenos Aires, Argentina
Attention: Jorge Marcelo Amodio
TEL: +541 313 8082
FAX: +541 814 4824
E-mail: pete@atina.ar
os@atina.ar
Area Served: Argentina

AT&T Mail
AT&T Mail Customer Assistance Center (ATTMAIL-DOM)
5000 Hadley Road
South Plainsfield, NJ 07080
TEL: 1 (800) MAIL-672 or   1-800-367-7225

in Canada (613) 778-5815
in UK or the Republic of Ireland
0800-289-403 or ++44-
527-67585
in Europe +322-676-3737
in Japan 81-3-5561-3411
in the Pacific Rim +852-846-2800
in Africa or the Americas +908-658-6175
E-mail: POSTMASTER@ATTMAIL.COM
Area Served: International
Service: Terminal; Client/Server; Busniess Services

BALTBONE

Ants Work
Deputy Director
Institute of Cybernetics
Estonian Academy of Sciences
Akadeemie tee 21
EE 0108 TALLINN
ESTONIA
TEL: +007 0142 525622
FAX: +007 0142 527901
E-mail: ants@ioc.ee
Area Served: Baltic countries: Estonia, Lithuania,
Latvia

BARRNet (Bay Area Regional Research Network)

Pine Hall Rm. 115
Stanford, CA 94305-4122
USA
Attn: William Yundt
TEL: +1 415 723 3104
E-mail: gd.why@forsythe.stanford.edu
Area Served: San Francisco Bay Area, Northern
California
Services: Network Connections; Terminal.

BCnet

BCnet Headquarters
515 West Hastings Street
Vancouver, British Columbia
Canada V6B 5K3
Attn: Mike Patterson
TEL: +1 604 291 5209
FAX: +1 604 291 5022
E-mail: Mike@bc.net
Area Served: British Columbia, Canada
Type of Service: Network Connections

BELNET (Belgian Research Network)

DPWB-SPPS
Wetenschapsstraat 8
B-1040 Brussels
Belgium
TEL: +32 2 238 3470
E-mail: helpdesk@belnet.be
Area Served: Belgium

BGnet

Daniel Kalchev
c/o Digital Systems
Neofit Bozveli 6
Varna—9000
BULGARIA
VOICE & FAX: +359 52 234540
E-mail: postmaster@Bulgaria.EU.net
Area Served: Bulgaria

The Black Box (blkbox.com)

P.O. Box 591822
Houston, TX 77259-1822
TEL: 713-480-2684 voice, 713-480-2686 modem
FAX: None
E-mail: info@blkbox.com

Area Served: Houston, Texas
Services: Terminal, UUCP, Personal IP, Network
Connections
Last Update: 4/5/94

CA*net

CA*net Information Centre
Computing Services
University of Toronto
4 Bancroft Ave., Rm. 116
Toronto, Ontario
CANADA, M5S 1A1
Attn: Eugene Siciunas
TEL: +1416 978 5058
FAX: +1 416 978 6620
E-mail: info@CAnet.ca
eugene@vm.utcs.utoronto.ca
Area Served: Canada

CARNet (Croatian Academic and Research Network)

J. Marohnica bb
41000 Zagreb
Croatia
TEL: +38 41 510 033
E-mail: helpdesk@carnet.hr
Area Served: Croatia

CCAN (Computer Communication Access for NGOs)

121/72 Soi Chalermla, Phya Thai Rd.,
Rajthevee, Bangkok 10400
Thailand
TEL: (66-2) 255-5552, 251-0704
FAX: (66-2) 255-5552
E-mail: ccan@peg.apc.org
Area Served: Thailand

CCI Networks, a division of Corporate Computers Inc.

4130—95 Street, Edmonton, AB, Canada, T6E 6H5
TEL: +1403 450 6787
FAX: +1 403 450 9143
E-mail: info@ccinet.ab.ca
Area Served: Edmonton, Alberta, Canada (1 Feb 1994)
Rest of Alberta during Q294
Services: Terminal, Personal IP, UUCP
Last Update: 3/24/94

CERFnet (California Education and Research Federation Network)

P.O. Box 85608
San Diego, CA 92186-9784
TEL: +1-800 876 2373 or +1 619 455 3900
FAX: +1 619 455 3990
E-mail: help@cerf.net
Area Served: California and International
Services: Network Connections; Terminal

CERN

CN Division
CH-1211 Geneva 23
Switzerland
TEL: +41 22 7673356
FAX: +41 22 7677155
E-mail: postmaster@cern.ch
C=ch;ADMD=arcom;PRMD=cern;O=cern;
S=Postmaster

Chasque

Casilla Correo 1539
Montevideo 11000
Uruguay
TEL: +598 (2) 496-192

FAX: +598 (2) 419-222
E-mail: apoyo@chasque.apc.org
Area Served: Uruguay & Paraguay
Services: Terminal, UUCP

CICNet (Committee on Institutional Cooperation Network)
ITI Building
2901 Hubbard Drive
Pod G
Ann Arbor, MI 48105
Attn: John Hankins
TEL: +1 313 998 6102
E-mail: hankins@cic.net
Area Served: Minnesota, Wisconsin, Iowa, Illinois, Indiana, Michigan, and Ohio
Services: Network Connections

Clark Internet Services
10600 Rt. 108
Ellicott City, MD 21045
VOICE: First dial Maryland Relay Service for hearing impaired at 1-800-735-2258 then ask operator for extension 410-730-9764
FAX: 410-730-9765
E-mail: info@clark.net (person)
all-info@clark.net (auto-reply info)
Area Served: Metro Maryland, District of Columbia, Northern Virginia
Services: Terminal, Network Connections
Last Update: 3/17/94

Clinet Ltd
PL 503/Tekniikantie 17
02150 Espoo
FINLAND
TEL: +358-0-4375209

FAX: +358-0-455 5276
E-mail: clinet@clinet.fi
Area Served: Finland
Services: Terminal
Last Update: 4/5/94

CNS (Community News Service)
1155 Kelly Johnson Blvd., Ste. 400
Colorado Springs, CO 80920
USA
TEL: +1 719 592 1240 or +1 800 748 1200
FAX: +1 719 592 1201
E-mail: service@cscns.com
Area Served: Colorado and US
Services: Terminal, UUCP, Business Services
Last Update: 2/24/94

Communications Accessibles Montreal (CAM.ORG)
TEL: +1 514-923-2102
E-mail: info@CAM.ORG
Area Served: Canada, QC: Montreal, Laval, South-Shore, West-Island (area code 514)
Services: Terminal

CONNECT
The IBM PC User Group
Attn: Alan Jay or Matther Farwell
P.O. Box 360
Harrow HA1 4LQ
ENGLAND
TEL: +44 0 81 863 1191
FAX: +44 0 81 863 6095
E-mail: info@ibmpcug.co.uk
Area served: London area

Cooperative Agency for Library Systems and Services (CLASS)
1415 Koll Circle
Suite 101
San Jose, CA 95112-4698
USA
TEL: +1-800 488 4559 or +1 408 453 0444
FAX: +1 408 453 5379
E-mail: class@class.org
Area Served: U.S.
Services: Terminal; Special: Access for libraries in the U.S.

COLNODO
Carrera 23 No. 39-82
Santafe de Bogota
Columbia
TEL: 57-2697181, 2444692, 2697202
E-mail: julian@colnodo.igc.apc.org
Area Served: Columbia

Colorado SuperNet
CSM Computing Center
Colorado School Mines
1500 Illinois
Golden, CO 80401
Attn: Ken Harmon
TEL: +1 303 273 3471
FAX: +1 303 273 3475
E-mail: kharmon@csn.org
info@csn.org
Area Served: Colorado
Services: Network Connections

ComLink
Emil-Meyer-Str. 20
D-30165 Hannover

GERMANY
TEL: +49 (511) 350-1573
FAX: +49 (511) 350-1574
E-mail: support@oln.comlink.apc.org
Area Served: Germany, Austria, Switzerland, Zagreb, Beograd
Services: Terminal, UUCP

Community News Service
1715 Monterey Road
Colorado Springs, CO 80910
USA
TEL: +1 719 579 9120
E-mail: klaus@cscns.com
Area Served: Colorado Springs (719 area code)
Services: Dialup Host.

CompuServe Information System
5000 Arlington Center Boulevard
P.O. Box 20212
Columbus, OH 43220
TEL: +1 614 457 0802 or +1-800 848 8990
E-mail: postmaster@csi.compuserve.com
Area Served: U.S. and International
Services: Personal Infortmation Service; Network Connections

CONCERT (Communications for North Carolina Education, Research, and Technology Network)
P.O. Box 12889
3021 Cornwallis Road
Research Triangle Park, NC 27709
USA
Attn: Joe Ragland
TEL: +1 919 248 1404
E-mail: jrr@concert.net
Area Served: North Carolina
Services: Network Connections, Terminal

Connect

Connect.com.au pty ltd
29 Fitgerald Crescent
Caulfield Victoria 3161
AUSTRALIA
TEL: +61 3 528 2239
FAX: +61 3 5285887
E-mail: connect@connect.com.au
Area Served: Australia: Melbourne, Sydney
Services: Dialup Host
Last Update: 2/24/94

CRL (CR Laboratories Dialup Internet Access)

TEL: +1 415 381 2800
E-mail: info@crl.com
Area Served: California (San Francisco Bay Area)
continental U.S./800
Services: Dialup Host

CRNet

National Academy of Sciences
Academia Nacional de Ciencias
San Jose
COSTA RICA
TEL: (506) 53 45 02
E-mail: gdeter@NS.CR
Area Served: Costa Rica (Acedemic, NGO, and R&D
communities)
Services: Terminal, Network Connections
Last Update: 4/5/95

CTS Network Services

A Division of Datel Systems, Inc.
4444 Convoy Street, Suite 300
San Diego CA 92111-3708
TEL: 619.637.3637
FAX: 619.637.3630

Data: 619.637.3660
E-mail: support@ctsnet.cts.com — human response
info@ctsnet.cts.com — automated response
Area Served: San Diego County (619)
Services: dialup-host, personal information services,
network connections, client/server services, UUCP,
business services, special services (including DNS,
IDR, custom domain aliasing)
Last Update: 2/23/94

CYBER (The Cyberspace Station)

E-mail: help@cyber.net
Area Served: CA: San Diego (area code 619)
Services: Dialup Host

CyberGate, Inc.

662 So. Military Trail
Deerfield Beach, FL 33442
USA
TEL: +1 305 428 4283
FAX: +1 305 428 7977
E-mail: sales@gate.net
Area Served: Southeast & Central Florida
Services: Terminal, Network Connections, Business
Services, UUCP
Last Update: 3/3/94

DASNET

DA Systems, Inc.
1053 East Campbell Avenue
Campbell, CA 95008
USA
TEL: +1 408 559 7434
Area Served: California and International
Services: Terminal; Special: E-mail connectivity
services

Data Basix

P.O. Box 18324
Tucson, AZ 85731
TEL: +1 602 721 1988
FAX: +1 602 721 7240
E-mail: Sales@Data.Basix.COM
RHarwood@Data.Basix.COM
Area Served: Tucson, Arizonia
Services: Terminal
Last Update: 2/3/94

DataNet

Telecom Finland
P.O. Box 228
Rautatienkatu 10
33101 TAMPERE
FINLAND
Attn: Seppo Noppari
TEL: +358 31 243 2242
FAX: +358 31 243 2211
E-mail: seppo.noppari@tele.fi
Area Served: Finland

DELPHI

General Videotex Corporation
1030 Massachusetts Ave.
Cambridge, MA 02138
TEL: +1 800 544 4005
E-mail: walthowe@delphi.com
Area Served: U.S.
Services: Terminal

DENet (The Danish Network for Research and Education UNI-C)

The Danish Computing Centre for Research and Education
Building 305, DTH

DK-2800 Lyngby
DENMARK
Attn: Jan P. Sorensen
TEL: +45 45 93 83 55
FAX: +45 45 93 02 20
E-mail: Jan.P.Sorensen@uni-c.dk
C=dk; ADMD=dk400; PRMD=minerva
O=UNI-C; S=Linden; G=Steen
Area Served: Denmark

DFN

DFN-Verein e. V.
Geschaeftsstelle
Pariser Strasse 44
D - 1000 Berlin 15
GERMANY
TEL: +49 30 88 42 99 22
FAX: +49 30 88 42 99 70
E-mail: dfn-verein@dfn.dbp.de
wilhelm@dfn.dbp.de
rauschenbach@dfn.dbp.de
Area Served: Germany

Direct Connection

P.O. Box 931
London SE18 3PW
England
TEL: +44 (0)81 317 0100
FAX: +44 (0)81 317 3886
E-mail: helpdesk@dircon.co.uk
Area Served: The UK (England)
Services: Terminal, UUCP
Last Update: 3/4/94

DKnet

EUnet in Denmark. See EUnet for further information.

DMConnection
Doyle Munroe Consultants, Inc.
267 Cox St.
Hudson, MA 01749
TEL: (508) 568-1618
FAX: (508) 562-1133
E-mail: postmaster@dmc.com
Area Served: New England
Type of Services: Network Connections, Terminal,
UUCP
Last Updated: 1/28/94

DPB
Research and Technology Centre
Section T 34
P. O. Box 10 00 03
D-W-6100 DARMSTADT
Germany
TEL: +49 6151 83 5210
FAX: +49 6151 83 4639
Email: G=walter; S=tietz; O=telekom; A=dbp; C=de
Area Served: Germany
Type of Services: X.400

EARN (European Academic Research Network)
BP 167
F-91403 Orsay CEDEX
FRANCE
TEL: +33 1 69 82 39 73
FAX: + 33 1 69 28 52 73
E-mail: grange%frors12.bitnet@mitvma.mit.edu
Area Served: Europe and International
Service: Network Connections

EARN-France
European Academic Research Network - FRANCE
950 rue de Saint Priest
34184 Montpellier Cedex 4

FRANCE
Attn: Dominique Dumas
TEL: +33 67 14 14 14
FAX: +33 67 52 57 63
E-mail
BRUCH%FRMOP11.BITNET@pucc.Princeton.EDU
BRUCH@FRMOP11.BITNET (Bitnet)
Area Served: France

ECONNECT
Sdruzeni Pro Snadne Spojeni
Naovcinach 2 170 00 Prague 7,
Czech Republic
TEL: +42(02) 66710366
E-mail: sysop@ecn.gn.apc.org
Area Served: Czech Republic

EcuaNex
12 de Octubre, Of. 504
Casilla 17-12-566
Quito
ECUADOR
TEL: +593 (2) 528-716
FAX: +593 (2) 505-073
E-mail: intercom@ecuanex.apc.org
Area Served: Ecuador
Services: Terminal, UUCP

ELCI
Box 72461
Nairobi
Kenya
TEL: +254 2 562 015 or +254 2 562 022
FAX: +254 2 562 175
E-mail: sysop@elci.gn.apc.org
Area Served: Kenya
Services: Terminal, UUCP

EMAIL CENTRE
108. V. Luna Road, Sikatuna Village
Quezon City
Philippines
TEL: +632 921 9976
E-mail: sysop@phil.gn.apc.org
Area Served: Philippines

ENDA
BP 3370
Dakar
Senegal
TEL: +221 21 6027 or +221 22 4229
FAX: +221 21 2695
E-mail: sysop@endadak.gn.apc.org
Area Served: Senegal
Services: Terminal, UUCP

ERNET (Education and Research Community Network)
Gulmohar Cross Road, Number 9
Juhu, Bombay 400 049
INDIA
TEL: +91 22 436 1329
FAX: +91 22 620 0590
E-mail: usis@doe.ernet.in
Area Served: India (Acedemic and R&D Communities)
Services: UUCP, Network Connection
Last Update: 4/5/94

Eskimo North
P.O. Box 75284
Seattle, WA 98125-0284
USA
E-mail: nanook@eskimo.com

Area Served: Seattle Washington Metro Area
Services: Terminal
Last Update: 3/1/94

EUNET
Kruislaan 409
1098 SJ Amsterdam
NETHERLANDS
TEL: +31 20 592 5109
FAX: +31 20 592 5155
FAX problems: +31 20 592 9444
E-mail: info@eu.net
Area Served: Europe and International (Algeria, Austria, Belgium, Bulgaria, Czech Republic, Denmark, Egypt, Finland, France, Germany, Greece, Hungary, Iceland, Ireland, Italy, Luxembourg, Morocco, Netherlands, Norway, Portugal, Romania, Slovakia, Slovenia, Russia and other parts of former Soviet Union, Spain, Switzerland, Tunisia, United Kingdom)
Service: Network Connections, UUCP.

EuropaNET
DANTE (Delivery of Advanced Network Technology to Europe Limited)
Lockton House
Clarendon Road
Cambridge, CB2 2BH
UK
TEL: +44 223 302 992
FAX: +44 223 303 005
E-mail: dante@dante.org.uk
Area Served: Europe (US, Canada, Rep. of Korea via provision of intercontinental lines)
Services: Network Connections, X.400, Special (connection to a continental backbone)

EVERGREEN COMMUNICATIONS Libre Service
5333 N. 7th Street, Suite B-220
Phoenix, AZ 85014
USA
TEL: +1(602) 230-9330
FAX: +1 (602) 230-9773
E-mail: jennyu@libre.com
Area Served: Arizona
(Phoenix, Tucson, Prescott, Casa Grande, Sierra Vista, Flagstaff) Nevada (Incline Village, NorthLake Tahoe, Reno, Carson City, Las Vegas) New Mexico (Albuquerque, Santa Fe) Mexico (Hispanic Events) Four Corners (NM,AZ,UT,NV) (Native American Events)
Services: Network Connections, Terminal, UUCP, Personal Information Services, Wireless
Last Update: 3/4/94

Express Access Online Communications Service (DIGEX)
Digital Express Group, Inc.
6006 Greenbelt Road #228
Greenbelt, MD 20770
USA
TEL: +1 301 220 2020
E-mail: info@digex.com
Area Served: Northern Virginia; Baltimore, Maryland; Washington, DC
(area codes 202, 310, 410, 703)
Services: Terminal

EZ-E-Mail
Shecora Associates, Inc.
P.O. Box 7604
Nashua, NH 03060
USA
TEL: +1 603 672 0736

E-mail: info@lemuria.sai.com
Area Served: U.S. and Canada
Services: Terminal

Fnet Sylvain Langlois
FNET Association
11 rue Carnot
94270 Le Kemlin-Bicetre
FRANCE
TEL: +33 1 45 21 02 04
FAX: +33 1 46 58 94 20
E-mail: contact@fnet.fr
Area Served: France

Freelance Systems Programming
807 Saint Nicholas Avenue
Dayton, OH 45410
USA
TEL: +1 513-254-7246
Data: +1 513-258-7745
E-mail: Tkellar@Dayton.fsp.com
Area Served: Dayton, Ohio
Services: Terminal
Last Update: 2/23/94

FUNET (Finnish University and Research Network)
P.O. Box 40
SF-02101 Espoo
FINLAND
Attn: Markus Sadeniemi
TEL: +358 0 457 2711
FAX: +358 0 457 2302
E-mail: sadeniemi@funet.fi
C=FI; O=FUNET; ADMD=fumail;
S=Sadeniemi; G=Markus;
Area Served: Finland

GARR (Gruppo Armonizzazione delle Reti per la Ricerca)
c/o CNR -Istituto Cnuce
Via S.Maria, 36
56126 Pisa
ITALY
TEL: +39 50 593360
FAX: +39 50 589354
E-mail: INFO@NIS.GARR.IT
C=IT; ADMD=GARR; PRMD=NIS; S=INFO
Area Served: Italy

GBnet
EUnet in Great Britain. See EUnet for further information.

GEONET
GeoNet Mailbox Systems
TEL: +49 6673 18881
E-mail: GmbH@geod.geonet.de
postmaster@geo5.geomail.org
Area Served: Germany

GLAIDS Internet BBS
P.O. Box 20771 Seattle WA 98102
TEL: 206-323-7483
E-mail: tomh@glaids.wa.com
Area Served: Internet/Seattle
Services: Terminal, UUCP
Last Update: 3/24/94

GlasNet
Ulitsa Sadovaya-Chernograizskaya
dom 4, Komnata 16, Third Floor
107078 Moscow
RUSSIA
TEL: +7 (095) 207-0704

FAX: +7 (095) 207-0889
E-mail: support@glas.apc.org
Area Served: Russia and other Commonwealth of Independent State's countries.
Services: Terminal, UUCP

Global Enterprise Service, Inc.
(was JvNCnet)
John von Neumann Center Network
6 von Neuman Hall
Princeton University
Princeton, NJ 08544
Attn: Sergio F. Heker or Allison Pihl
TEL: +1 609 258 2400 or +1-800 358 4437
E-mail: market@jvnc.net
Area Served: U.S. and International
Services: Network Connections, Terminal

GLUK—GlasNet-Ukraine, Ltd
14b Metrologicheskaya str.
Kiev, 252143 Ukraine
TEL: +7 (044) 266 9481
FAX: +7 (044) 266 9475
E-mail: support@gluk.apc.org
Area Served: Ukraine
Services: Terminal, UUCP

GreenNet
23 Bevenden Street
London N1 6BH
UNITED KINGDOM
TEL: +44 (71) 608 3040
FAX: +44 (71) 253 0801
E-mail: support@gn.apc.org
Area Served: International, Africa
Services: Special: FTS (FidoNet) Polling Services

Halcyon

Dataway
P.O. Box 555
Grapeview, WA 98546-0555
TEL: +1 206 426 9298
E-mail: info@remote.halcyon.com
Area Served: Seattle, Washington
Services: Terminal.

HEANET

Higher Education Authority
Fitzwilliam Square, Dublin
IRELAND
Attn: Mike Norris   or   John Hayde
TEL: +353 1 612748 (Norris)   +353 1 761545 (Hayden)
FAX: +353 1 610492
E-mail: Mnorris@hea.ie   jhayden@vax1.tcd.ie
C-ie; ADMD=Eirmail400; PRMD=NRN; O=hes; S=mnorris
Area Served: Ireland

HISTRIA (ABM-BBS)

Ziherlova 43 61
Ljubljana, Slovenia
TEL: + 38 61 211-553
FAX: + 38 61 152-107
E-mail: support@histria.apc.org
Area Served: Slovenia

HoloNet

Information Access Technologies, Inc.
TEL: +1 510 704 0160
FAX: +1 510 704 8019
E-mail: info@holonet.net
Area Served: Berkeley, California (area code 510)
Services: Terminal.

Hong Kong Supernet

HKUST Campus
Clear Water Bay, Kowloon
HONG KONG
TEL: (+852)358-7924
FAX: (+852)358-7925
E-mail: info@hk.super.net
Area Served: Hong Kong and the ASEAN region
Services: Terminal, Network Connections, Client/Server, UUCP
Last Update: 2/23/94

HookUp Communications

1075 North Service Road West
Suite 207
Oakville, Ontario, L6M 2G2
TEL: (905) 847-8000
FAX: (905) 847-8420
E-mail: info@hookup.net
Area Served: Ontario Canada, Canada-wide (through 1-800 service)
Services: Terminal
Last Update: 4/5/94

HUNGARNET

Computer and Automation Institute
H-1132 Budapest
18-22 Victory Hugo
HUNGARY
Attn: Istvan Tetenyi
TEL: +36 11497352
E-mail: postmaster@ella.hu
Area Served: Hungary

IDS World Network Internet Access Service

3 Franklin Road
East Greenwich, RI 02818

TEL: +1 (401) 884-7856
E-mail: info@ids.net
Area Served: Local Access in Rhode Island and Miami, Florida
Services: Terminal, UUCP, Personal IP
Last Update: 4/5/94

IEunet

EUnet in Ireland. See EUnet for further information.

ILAN Israeli Academic Network Information Center

Computer Center
Tel Aviv University
ISRAEL
Attn: Ramat Aviv
TEL: +972 3 6408309
E-mail: hank@vm.tau.ac.il
Area Served: Israel

INCA

Internetworking Cape
P.O. Box 6844
Roggebaai 8012
SOUTH AFRICA
TEL: +27 21 4192690
E-mail: info@inca.za
Area Served: South Africa
Services: Network Connections, Terminal, UUCP

INDIALINK BOMBAY

Praveen Rao, Indialink Coord. Bombay
c/o Maniben Kara Institute
Nagindas Chambers, 167 P.D'Mello Rd
Bombay—400 038
TEL: 91-22-262-2388 or 261-2185
E-mail: mki@inbb.gn.apc.org
Area Served: India

INDIALINK DELHI

Leo Fernandez, Coordinator Indialink
c/o Indian Social Institute
10 Institutional area, Lodiroad,
New Delhi
TEL: 91-11-463-5096 or 461-1745
FAX:91-11-462-5015
E-mail: leo@unv.ernet.in
Area Served: India

Individual Network e.V.

TEL: none
FAX: 02238/2593
E-mail: IN-Info@Individual.net
Area Served: Germany: Berlin, Flensburg, Kiel, Hamburg, Bremen, Oldenburg, Muenster, Osnabrueck, Hannover, Braunschweig, Kassel, Dortmund, Magdeburg, Jena, Chemnitz, Dresden, Rostock, Aachen, Duisburg, Wuppertal, Koeln, Bonn, Kaarst, Duesseldorf, Frankfurt, Saarbruecken, Nuernberg, Ulm, Wuerzburg, Muenchen, Konstanz
Services: Network Connections, UUCP, Personal IP
Last Update: 3/23/94

INet

University Computing Services
Wrubel Computing Center
Indiana University
750 N. State Rd. 46
Bloomington, IN 47405
Attn: Dick Ellis
TEL: +1 812 855 4240
E-mail: ellis@ucs.indiana.edu
Area Served: Indiana
Services: Network Connections.

InfiNet, L.C.
Internet Communications Services
211 East City Hall Avenue, Suite 236
Norfolk, VA 23510
USA
TEL: +1 804 622-4289
FAX: +1 804 622-7158
E-mail: rcork@infi.net
Area Served: Tidwater Virginia area,
USA via Compuserve Packet
Network
Services: Terminal, UUCP

Infolan
Infonet Service Corporation
2100 East Grand Avenue
El Segundo, CA 90245
Attn: George Abe
TEL: +1 310 335 2600
FAX: +1 310 335 2876
E-mail: abe@infonet.com
Area Served: International, including U.S. Europe,
Canada, Hong Kong, Japan, Singapore, and Australia.

Institute for Global Communications (IGC)
(ECONET, PEACENET, CONFLICTNET, LABORNET)
18 De Boom Street
San Francisco, CA 94107
USA
TEL: +1 415 442 0220
FAX: +1 415 546 1794   TELEX: 154205417
E-mail: support@igc.apc.org
Area served: International
Services: Terminal; UUCP: Polling service

InterAccess
9400 W. Foster Ave.
Suite 111

Chicago, IL 60656
TEL: 800-967-1580
FAX: 708-671-0113
E-mail: info@interaccess.com
Area Served: Chicagoland
Services: Terminal, UUCP, Personal IP, Network
Connections
Last Update: 4/5/94

Internet Consult
abraxas dataselskab a/s
International House - Bella Center
2300 Koebenhavn S
DENMARK
TEL: +45 32 47 33 55
FAX: +45 32 47 30 16
E-mail: <info@ic.dk>
Area Served: Denmark
Services: UUCP, Personal IP
Last Update: 4/5/94

Internet Direct, Inc.
1366 East Thomas, Suite 210
Phoenix, AZ 85014
USA
TEL: (602)274-0100
FAX: (602)274-8518
E-mail: info@indirect.com
Area Served: Arizona
Service: Terminal
Last Updated: 1/28/94

InterNex Information Services, Inc.
1050 Chestnut St. Suite 202
Menlo Park, CA 94025
TEL: 415-473-3060
FAX: 415-473-3062
E-mail: info@internex.net

Area Served: San Francisco Bay Area
Services: Network Connection via ISDN, Client/
Server
Last Update: 4/5/94

Internex Online (Io)
1 Yonge Street Suite 1801
Toronto, Ontario Canada
M5E 1W7
TEL: 416 363-8676 (VOICE); 416 363-4151 (online
registration/info)
FAX: 416 369-0515
E-mail:: vid@io.org
Area Served: Toronto, Ontario, Canada
Services: Terminal
Last Update: 3/17/94

Ireland On-Line
West Wing, Udaras Complex
Furbo
Galway Ireland
Attn: Barry Flanagan <barryf@iol.ie>
TEL: +353 91 92727
FAX: +353 91 92726
E-mail: postmaster@iol.ie
Area Served: Ireland
Services: Terminal, Personal Information Services,
Network Connections

ISnet
c/o SURIS
University of Iceland
Dunhaga 5
107 Reykjavik
ICELAND
Attn: Marius Olafsson
TEL: +354 1 694747

E-mail: marius@rhi.hi.is
C=is; ADMD=0; PRMD=isaneet; O=hi; OU=rhi;
S=marius
Area Served: Iceland

ITALYNET
Via G.Taddei 3
Pisa, Italy
TEL: 39-5-57-6343
E-mail: cesare@gn.apc.org
Area Served: Italy

ITESM
Depto. de Telecomunicaciones y Redes
ITESM Campus Monterrey
E. Garza Sada #2501
Monterrey, N.L., C.P. 64849
MEXICO
Attn: Ing. Hugo E. Garcia Torres
TEL: +52 83 582 000 ext. 4130
FAX: +52 83 588 931
E-mail: hugo@mtecv1.mty.itesm.mx
Area Served: Mexico

IUnet
Alessandro Berni
DIST, Universita' di Genova
Via Opera Pia, 11A
16145 Genova
ITALY
TEL: +39 10 353 2747
FAX: +39 10 353 2948
E-mail: ab@dist.unige.it
Area Served: Italy

JANET (Joint Academic Network)
JANET Liaison Desk

c/o Rutherford Appleton Laboratory
GB-Oxon OX11 OQX
UNITED KINGDOM
Attn: Chilton Didcot
TEL: +44 235 5517
E-mail: JANET-LIAISON-DESK@jnt.ac.uk
O=GB;ADMD=; PRMD=uk.ac; O=jnt;
G=JANET-LIAISON-DESK; (X.400)
Area Served: United Kingdom

JARING
MIMOS
7th Flr, Exchange Square
Off Jalan Semantan
50490 Kuala Lumpur, MALAYSIA
TEL: +60-3-254-9601 or +60-3-255-2700 ext 2101
FAX: +60-3-253-1898 or +60-3-255-2755
E-mail: noc@jaring.my
Area Served: Malaysia
Services: Terminal, UUCP, Network Connections

JIPS Joint Network Team
c/o Rutherford Appleton Laboratory
Chilton Didcot
Oxon OX11 0QX
UNITED KINGDOM
Attn: Dr. Bob Day
TEL: +44 235 44 5163
E-mail: r.a.day@jnt.ac.uk
Area Served: United Kingdom

KAIWAN Corporation
12550 Brookhurst, Garden Grove, CA 92640
TEL: +1 714-638-2139
FAX: +1 714-638-0455
E-mail: info@kaiwan.com
Area Served: Southern California

Services: UUCP,Terminal, Personal Information
Services, Network Connections, Client/
Server,Wireless,Business Services
Last Update: 3/17/94

Kuentos Communications, Inc.
P.O. Box 26870
GMF Guam 96921
TEL: 671-637-5488
FAX: 671-632-5641
E-mail: pkelly@Kuentos.Guam.NET
Area Service: Guam
Services: Termainal, UUCP, Personal IP, Network
Connections
Last Update: 4/5/94

LANETA
Tlalpan 1025, col. portales
Mexico, df. Mexico
TEL: (525) 2774791, (525) 5755395
FAX: (525) 277-4791
E-mail: soporte@laneta.igc.apc.org
Area Served: Mexico

Latvian Internet Centre
University of Latvia, Institute of Computer Science
Rainis Blvd. 29
Riga LV-1459
LATVIA
TEL: +371 2 224730 or +371 2 212427
FAX: +371 8 820153
E-mail: postmaster@mii.lu.lv
Area Served: Latvia
Services: Network Connections, Terminals, UUCP,
USENet News

Lega per L'Ambiente
via Salaria 280
I-00194 Roma
ITALY
TEL: +39/6-844-2277
E-mail: legambiente@gn.apc.org
Area Served: Italy

Los Nettos
University of Southern California
Information Sciences Institute
4676 Admiralty Way
Marina del Rey, CA 90292
Attn: Ann Westine Cooper
TEL: +1 310 822 1511
E-mail: los-nettos-request@isi.edu
Area Served: Los Angeles Area, Southern California
Services: Network Connections

LvNet-Teleport
204 Brivibas str
Riga, LV-1039
Latvia
TEL: +371 2551133
FAX: +371 2553261
E-mail: vit@lynx.riga.lv
Area Served: Latvia
Services: Network Connections, UUCP, Special (FTP-email gateway and Fax-email gateway)

Maestro Technologies, Inc.
29 John Street Suite 1601
New York, NY 10038
USA
TEL: +1 212 240 9600
E-mail: info@maestro.com
Area Served: New York

Services: Terminal
Last Update: 2/3/94

MANGO
P.O. Box 7069
Harare, Zimbabwe
TEL: +263 4 303 211 EXT 1492
Email: sysop@mango.apc.org
Area Served: Zimbabwe

MBnet
Director, Computing Services
University of Manitoba
603 Engineering Building
Winnipeg, Manitoba
CANADA, R3T 2N2
Attn: Gerry Miller
TEL: +1 204 474 8230
FAX: +1 204 275 5420
E-mail: miller@ccm.UManitoba.ca
Area Served: Manitoba, Canada

MCI Mail
1133 19th Street, NW
7th Floor
Washington, DC 20036
TEL: +1-800 444 6245   or   +1 202 833 8484
E-mail: 2671163@mcimail.com
3248333@mcimail.com
Area Served: U.S. and International
Services: Terminal; Client/Server; Special: Business Services like FAX available

MichNet/Merit
2200 Bonisteel Blvd.
Ann Arbor, MI 48109-2112
Attn: Jeff Ogden

TEL: +1 313 764 9430
E-mail: info@merit.edu
Area Served: Michigan
Services: Network Connections; Terminal

MIDnet

Midwestern States Network
29 WSEC
University of Nebraska
Lincoln, NE 68588
Attn: Dale Finkelson
TEL: +1 402 472 5032
E-mail: dmf@westie.unl.edu
Area Served: Midwestern States, including Iowa,
Kansas, Oklahoma, Arkansas, Missouri, South
Dakota, and Nebraska
Services: Network Connections

Milwaukee Internet X

Mix Communications
P.O. Box 17166
Milwaukee, WI 53217
TEL: +1 414 962 8172
E-mail: sysop@mixcom.com
Area Served: Milwaukee, Wisconsin
Services: Dialup Host

MindVox

Phantom Access Technologies, Inc.
175 Fifth Avenue, Suite 2614
New York, NY 10011
USA
TEL: +1 800 - MindVox or +1 212 989 2418
FAX: +1 212 989 8648
E-mail: postmaster@phantom.com
Area Served: New York
Services: Terminal
Last Update: 2/4/94

Mordor International BBS

TEL: +1 201 432-0600 (data)
FAX: +1 201 433-4222
E-mail: ritz@mordor.com
Area Served: New Jersey
Services: Terminal
Last Update: 3/17/94

MRnet

Minnesota Regional Network
511 11th Avenue South, Box 212
Minneapolis, MN 55415
Attn: Dennis Fazio
TEL: +1 612 342 2570
E-mail: dfazio@mr.net
Area Served: Minnesota
Services: Network Connections

MSEN, Inc.

628 Brooks Street
Ann Arbor, MI 48103
Attn: Owen Scott Medd
TEL: +1 313 998 4562
FAX: +1 313 998 4563
E-mail: info@msen.com
Area Served: U.S.
Services: Network Connections, Terminal

MUKLA

Makerere University
Kampala, Uganda
TEL: +256-41-532-479
E-mail: sysop@mukla.gn.apc.org
Area Served: Uganda
Services: Terminal, UUCP

MV Communications, Inc.

P.O. Box 4963
Manchester, NH 03108-4963
USA
TEL: (603) 429-2223
E-mail: mv-admin@mv.MV.COM
Area Served: New Hampshire
Services: Terminal
Last Update: 2/3/94

NB*net

Director, Computing Services
University of New Brunswick
Fredericton, New Brunswick
CANADA, E3B 5A3
Attn: David Macneil
TEL: +1 506 453 4573
FAX: +1 506 453 3590
E-mail: DGM@unb.ca
Area Served: New Brunswick, Canada

NEARnet

New England Academic and Research Network
BBN Systems and Technologies
10 Moulton Street
Cambridge, MA 02138
TEL: +1 617 873 8730
E-mail: nearnet-staff@nic.near.net
Area Served: Maine, Vermont, New Hampshire, Connecticut, Massachusetts, Rhode Island
Services: Network Connections, Terminal

NeoSoft

3408 Mangum
Houston, TX 77092
USA
TEL: +1 713 684-5969
FAX:
E-mail: info@NeoSoft.com
Area Served: Houston, Texas
Services: Terminal, Network Connections, UUCP
Last update: 3/1/94

Netcom Online Communication Services

P.O. Box 20774
San Jose, CA 95160
TEL: +1 408 554 8649
E-mail: info@netcom.com
Area Served: California
Services: Terminal

netILLINOIS

University of Illinois
Computing Services Office
1304 W. Springfield
Urbana, IL 61801
Attn: Joel L. Hartmann
TEL: +1 309 677 3100
E-mail: joel@bradley.bradley.edu
Area Served: Illinois
Services: Network Connections

netmbx

Feuerbachstr. 47/49, D-12163 Berlin
TEL: +49 30 855 53 50
FAX: +49 30 855 53 95
E-mail: netmbx@netmbx.de
Area Served: Berlin (Germany)
Services: Terminal, Personal Information Services, Network Connections, Client/Server, UUCP
Last Update: 3/4/94

NETSYS COMMUNICATION SERVICES
992 San Antonio Rd
Palo Alto, CA 94303
USA
TEL: +1 415 424 0384
E-mail: info@netsys.com
Area Served: Palo Alto, California
Types of Service: Terminal
Last Update: 1/28/94

NevadaNet
University of Nevada System
Computing Services
4505 Maryland Parkway
Las Vegas, NV 89154
Attn: Don Zitter
TEL: +1 702 784 6133
E-mail: zitter@nevada.edu
Area Served: Nevada
Services: Network Connections.

Nicarao
CRIES
Iglesia Carmen
1 cuadra al lago
Apartado 3516
Managua
NICARAGUA
TEL: +505 (2) 621-312
FAX: +505 (2) 621-244
E-mail: support@ni.apc.org
Area Served: Central America, Panama
Services: Terminal, UUCP

NLnet
Newfoundland and Labrador Network
Department of Computing and Communications
Memorial University of Newfoundland

St. John's, Newfoundland
CANADA, A1C 5S7
Attn: Wilf Bussey <wilf@morgan.ucs.mun.ca>
TEL: +1 709 737 8329
FAX: +1 709 737 3514
E-mail: admin@nlnet.nf.ca
Area Served: Newfoundland and Labrador, Canada
Type of Services: Terminal, Network Connections

NLnet
EUnet in the Netherlands. See EUnet for further information.

NordNet
Huvudskaersvaegen 13, nb
S-121 54 Johanneshov
SWEDEN
TEL: +46-8-6000331
FAX: +46-8-6000443
E-mail: support@pns.apc.org
Area Served: Sweden

NORDUNET
c/o SICS P.O. Box 1263
S-164 28 Kista
SWEDEN
TEL: +46 8 752 1563
FAX: +46 8 751 7230
E-mail: NORDUNET@sics.se
Area Served: Norway, Denmark, Finland, Iceland, Sweden

North Shore Access
A service of Eco Software, Inc.
145 Munroe Street, Suite 405
Lynn, MA 01901
USA

TEL: +1 617 593 3110
FAX: +1 617 593 3110
E-mail: info@northshore.ecosoft.com
Area Served: Boston Massachusetts and Eastern Massachusetts
Services: Terminal, UUCP
Last Update: 1/28/94

NorthWestNet

Northwestern States Network
NorthWestNet
2435 233rd Place NE
Redmond, WA 98053
Attn: Eric Hood
TEL: +1 206 562 3000
E-mail: ehood@nwnet.net
Area Served: Academic and research sites in Alaska, Idaho, Montana, North Dakota, Oregon, Wyoming, and Washington
Services: Network Connections

NSTN Nova Scotia Technology Network

General Manager, NSTN Inc.
900 Windmill Road, Suite 107
Dartmouth, Nova Scotia
CANADA, B3B 1P7
Attn: Mike Martineau
TEL: +1 902 468 6786
FAX: +1 902 468 3679
E-mail: martinea@hawk.nstn.ns.ca
Area Served: Nova Scotia, Canada

NTG/Xlink

Vincenz-Priessnitz-Str.3
D-76131 KARLSRUHE
GERMANY
TEL: +49 721 9652 0

FAX: +49 721 9652 210
E-mail: info@xlink.net
Area Served: Germany
Services: Network Connections, UUCP, Terminal,
Special: PSI-Mail
Last Update: 3/17/94

NYSERnet

New York State State Education and Research Network
200 Elwood Davis Road
Liverpool, NY 13088-6147
USA
TEL: +1 315 453 2912
E-mail: info@nysernet.org
Area Served: New York State and International
Services: Network Connections, Terminal, Personal IP
Last Update: 4/5/94

OARnet

Ohio Academic Research Network
Ohio Supercomputer Center
1224 Kinnear Road
Columbus, OH 43085
Attn: Alison Brown
TEL: +1 614 292 8100
E-mail: nic@oar.net
Area Served: Ohio
Services: Network Connections, Terminal

OLD COLORADO CITY COMMUNICATIONS

2502 W. Colorado Ave. # 204
Colorado Springs, CO 80904
USA
TEL: +1 719-593-7575 or +1 719-632-4848
FAX: +1 719-593-7521
E-mail: thefox@oldcolo.com or dave@oldcolo.com

Area Served: Colorado Springs
Services: Terminal
Last Update: 3/1/94

ONet ONet Computing Services
University of Toronto
4 Bancroft Avenue, Rm. 116
Toronto, Ontario,
CANADA, M5S 1A1
Attn: Eugene Siciunas
TEL: +1 416 978 5058
FAX: +1 416 978 6620
E-mail: eugene@vm.utcs.utoronto.ca
Area Served: Ontario,Canada
Services: Network Connections

Opus One
1404 East Lind Road
Phoenix, AZ
TEL: +1 602 324 0494
FAX: +1 602 324 0495
E-mail: info@opus1.com (machine)
jms@opus1.com (person)
Area Served: Arizona
Services: Terminal, Network connections
Last Updated: 3/1/94

ORSTOM—Institut Francais de Recherche Scientifique pour le Developpement en Cooperation Service Informatique
213, rue La Fayette
75480-PARIS-Cedex
FRANCE
TEL: +33 48037609   +33 67617510
E-mail: renaud@PARIS.ORSTOM.FR
michaux@ORSTOM.FR
Services: UUCP
Last Update: 1/28/94

OSLONETT Aksess
Gaustadalleen 21
N-0371 Oslo
NORWAY
TEL: +47 22 46 10 99
FAX: +47 22 46 45 28
E-mail: oslonett@oslonett.no
Area Served: Norway
Services: Terminal
Last Update: 1/28/94

OTC Electronic Trading
41 Mc Laren Street
North Sydney,
NSW 2060
Australia
TEL: +61 2 954 3055
FAX: +61 2 957 1406
E-mail: G=russell; S=fitzpatrick; O=et;
P=easicom;A=otc; C=au
S=helpdest; O=operations; P=enhanced;
A=otc; C=au
Area Served: Australia
Type of Services: X.400

PACCOM
University of Hawaii
Department of ICS
2565 The Mall
Honolulu, HI 96822
USA
Attn: Torben Nielsen
TEL: +1 808 949 6395
E-mail: torben@foralie.ics.hawaii.edu
Area Served: Pacific rim: Australia, Japan, Korea,
New Zealand, Hong Kong, Hawaii

Pacific Systems Group (RAINet)
9501 S.W. Westhaven
Portland, OR 97225
USA
TEL: (503) 297-8820
E-mail: rain-admin@psg.com

PACTOK
P.O. Box 284
Broadway 4006
Queensland, Australia
TEL: +61(7)257-1111
FAX: +61(7)257-1087
E-mail: pactok@peg.apc.org
Area Served: Pacific Islands

PADIS
Pan African Development Information System
Box 3001
Addis Ababa, Ethiopia
TEL: +251(1)511 167
FAX: +251(1)514 416
E-mail: sysop@padis.gn.apc.org
Area Served: Ethiopia
Services: Terminal, UUCP

PageSat, Inc.
8300 NE Underground Drive
Suite 430
Kansas City, MS 64161-9767
TEL: 800-989-7351 or 800-TYRELL-1
FAX: 816-741-5315
E-mail: root@tyrell.net
Area Served: U.S.
Services: Network Connections, Terminal, UUCP, Personal Information Services, Business Services

Panix Public Access Unix
c/o Alexis Rosen
110 Riverside Drive
New York, NY 10024
TEL: +1 212 877 4854 or +1 718 965 3768
E-mail: alexis@panix.com
jsb@panix.com
Area Served: New York City, New York
Services: Dialup Host, UUCP

PEACESAT Pan Pacific Education and Communications Experiments by Satellite
Social Science Research Institute
University of Hawaii at Manoa
Old Engineering Quad, Building 31
Honolulu, HI 96822
TEL: +1 808 956-7794/8848
FAX: +1 808 956 2512
E-mail: peacesat@uhunix.uhcc.hawaii.edu
Area served: Pan Pacific region
Service: Special—Satellite stations with E-mail, network, and voice capability

Pegasus Networks
P.O. Box 284
Broadway 4006
Queensland
AUSTRALIA
TEL: +61 (7) 257-1111
FAX: +61 (7) 257-1087
E-mail: support@peg.apc.org
Area Served: Australia, Pacific Islands, Southeast Asia
Services: Terminal, UUCP

Performance Systems International, Inc. (PSI)
11800 Sunrise Valley Drive
Suite 1100

Reston, VA 22091
TEL: +1 800 827 7482 or +1 703 620 6651
FAX: +1 703 620 4586
E-mail: info@psi.com
Area Served: U.S. and International
Services: Network Connections, UUCP, Client/Server

Pingnet
abraxas dataselskab a/s
International House—Bella Center
2300 Koebenhavn S
DENMARK
TEL: +45 32 47 33 93
FAX: +45 32 47 30 16
E-mail: adm@ping.dk
Area Served: Denmark
Services: UUCP
Last Update: 4/5/94

Pioneer Neighborhood
20 Moore St. #3
Somerville, MA 02144-2124
USA
TEL: +1 617 646 4800
E-mail: admin@pn.com
autoreply@pioneer.ci.net
Area Served: Boston, Massachusetts
Services: UUCP
Last Update: 2/4/94

The Pipeline
150 Broadway, Suite 1710
New York, NY 10038
USA
TEL: (212) 267-3636
E-mail: infobot@pipeline.com

Area Served: New York and International
Services: Terminal, Client/Server
Last Update: 1/28/94

PIPEX
Unipalm Ltd.
Michael Howes (sales information)
Richard Nuttall (technical information)
TEL: +44 223 424616
FAX: +44 223 426868
E-mail: pipex@unipalm.co.uk
Area served: United Kingdom

Piroska Giese KFKI-Research Institute for Particle and Nuclear Physics
H-1121 Budapest
Konkoly Thege ut 29-33
HUNGARY
TEL: (36-1) 169-9499
FAX: (36-1) 169-6567
E-mail: Piroska.Giese@rmki.kfki.hu
Area Served: Hungary, High Energy Physics Community
Services: Terminal, Personal Information Services Network Connections (dial-up and dedicated network links to regional, national, and international networks)

Prince Edward Island Network
University of Prince Edward Island
Computer Services
550 University Avenue
Charlottetown, P.E.I.
CANADA, C1A 4P3
Attn: Jim Hancock
TEL: +1 902 566 0450

FAX: +1 902 566 0958
E-mail: hancock@upei.ca
Area Served: Prince Edward Island, Canada

Portal Communications, Inc.
20863 Stevens Creek Blvd.
Suite 200
Cupertino, CA 95014
TEL: +1 408 973 9111
E-mail: cs@cup.portal.com
info@portal.com
Area Served: Northern California
Services: Terminal

PREPnet Pennsylvania Research and Economic Partnership Network
305 South Craig Street, 2nd Floor
Pittsburgh, PA 15213-3706
Attn: Thomas W. Bajzek
TEL: +1 412 268 7870
E-mail: twb+@andrew.cmu.edu
Area Served: Pennsylvania
Services: Network Connections

Prometheus Information Network Group, Inc.
Suite 284
4514 Chamblee Dunwoody Road
Dunwoody, GA 30338
USA
TEL: +1 404 818 6300
FAX: +1 404 458 8031
E-mail: questions@ping.com
Area Served: Georgia
Services: Network Connctions, Terminal, UUCP
Last Update: 2/3/94

PSCNET
Pittsburgh Supercomputing Center Network
Pittsburgh Supercomputing Center
4400 5th Avenue
Pittsburgh, PA 15213
Attn: Eugene Hastings
TEL: +1 412 268 4960
E-mail: pscnet-admin@psc.edu
Area Served: Eastern U.S. (Pennsylvania, Ohio, and West Virginia)
Services: Network Connections.

RARE
RARE Secretariat
Singel 466-468
NL-1017 AW
Amsterdam
NETHERLANDS
TEL: +31 20 639 1131
FAX: +31 20 639 3289
E-mail: raresec@rare.nl
Area Served: Europe
Services: Network Connections

RCCN Vasco Freitas
CCES
Universidade do Minho
Largo do Paco
P-4719 Braga Codex
PORTUGAL
Attn: Dr. Vasco Freitas
TEL: +351 53 612257
E-mail: vf@ce.fccn.pt
C=pt; ADMD= ; PRMD=fccn; O=ce; S=Freitas; G=Vasco;
Area Served: Portugal

RED400

Serge Aumont
CICB
Campus de Beaulieu
35042 Rennes
FRANCE
or
Paul-Andre Pays
INRIA
Domaine De Voluceau
Rocquencourt
BP 105
78150 Le Chesnay Cedex
FRANCE
TEL: +33 1 39 63 54 58
E-mail: contact-red@cicb.fr
C=FR; ADMD=atlas; PRMD=cicb; S=contact-red;
Area Served: France

REDID

Asesor Cientifico Union Latina
APTD0 2972
Santo Domingo
REPUBLIC DOMINICANA
Attn: Daniel Pimienta
TEL: +1 809 689 4973 or +1 809 535 6614
FAX:+18095356646
TELEX: 1 346 0741
E-mail: pimienta!daniel@redid.org.do
Area Served: Dominican Republic

RedIRIS

Secretaria RedIRIS
Fundesco
Alcala 61
28014 Madrid
SPAIN

TEL: +34 1 435 1214
FAX: +34 1 578 1773
E-mail: secretaria@rediris.es
C=es; ADMD=mensatex; PRMD=iris; O=rediris;
S=secretari   (X.400)
Area Served: Spain

Relcom

Demos
6 Ovchinnikovskaya nab.
113035 Moscow
RUSSIA
TEL: +7 095 231 2129 or +7 095 231 6395
FAX: +7 095 233 5016
E-mail: postmaster@hq.demos.su
info@hq.demos.su
Area Served: Russia

RESTENA

6 Rue Coudenhove Kalergi
L-1359
LUXEMBOURG
Attn: Antoine Barthel
TEL: +352 424409
E-mail: admin@restena.lu
C=lu; ADMD=pt; PRMD=restena; O=restena;
S=admin

RISCnet

InteleCom Data Systems
11 Franklin Road
East Greenwich, RI 02818
Attn: Andy Green
TEL: +1 401 885 6855
E-mail: info@nic.risc.net
Area Served: Rhode Island, New England
Services: Network Connections, Terminal

RISQ

Reseau Interordinateurs Scientifique Quebecois
Centre de Recherche Informatique de Montreal
(CRIM)
3744, Jean-Brillant, Suite 500
Montreal, Quebec
CANADA, H3T 1P1
Attn: Bernard Turcotte
TEL: +1 514 340 5700
FAX: +1 514 340 5777
E-mail: turcotte@crim.ca
Area Served: Quebec, Canada

SANET (Slovak Academic NETwork)

Vypoctove stredisko SAV
Dubravska cesta 9
842 35 Bratislava
Slovakia
TEL: +42 (7) 374422
E-mail: bobovsky@savba.cs
Area Served: Slovakia

SANGONET

13th floor Longsbank Building
187 Bree Street
Johannesberg 2000
South Africa
TEL: +27 (11) 838-6944
FAX: +27 (11) 838-6310
E-mail: support@wn.apc.org
Area Served: South Africa
Services: Terminal, UUCP

SASK#net

Computing Services
56 Physics
University of Saskatchewan

Saskatoon, Saskatchewan
CANADA, S7N 0W0
Attn: Dean Jones
TEL: +1 306 966 4860
FAX: +1 306 966 4938
E-mail: dean.jones@usask.ca
Area Served: Saskatchewan, Canada
Services: Netrwork Connections, Terminal, UUCP

SatelLife

Associate Director of Operations
SatelLife-U.S.A.,
126 Rogers Street
Cambridge, MA 02142 U.S.A.
Attn: Jon Metzger
TEL: (617) 868-8522
FAX: (617) 868-6647
E-mail: pnsatellife@igc.apc.org
Area Served: International Medical Community

SatelNET

2269 S. University Drive, Box 159
Davie, FL 33324
USA
Tel: +1 (305) 434 7340
FAX: +1 (305) 680-9848
E-mail: root@satelnet.org
Area Served: South-East Florida
Services: Terminal
Last Update: 3/4/94

SDSCnet

San Diego Supercomputer Center Network
San Diego Supercomputer Center
P.O. Box 85608
San Diego, CA 92186-9784
Attn: Paul Love

TEL: +1 619 534 5043
E-mail: loveep@sds.sdsc.edu
Area Served: San Diego Area, Southern California
Services: Network Connections

Seicom Computer GmbH/NO Carrier e.V

P.O. Box 7165
72784 PFULLINGEN
GERMANY
TEL: +49 7121 9770-0
FAX: +49 7121 9770-19
E-mail: info@seicom.de / no-carrier@schwaben.de
Area Served: Southern Germany { Tuebingen (07071), Reutlingen (07121), Stuttgart (0711)
Services: Terminal, Network Connection, UUCP, X.400
Last Update: 3/17/94

SESQUINET

Texas Sesquicentennial Network
Office of Networking and Computing Systems
Rice University
Houston, TX 77251-1892
Attn: Farrell Gerbode
TEL: +1 713 527 4988
E-mail: farrell@rice.edu
Area Served: Texas
Services: Network Connections

South Coast Computing Services, Inc.

P.O. Box 270355
Houston, TX 77277-0355
USA
TEL: +1 713-661-3301
FAX: +1 713-661-0633
E-mail: info@sccsi.com
Area Served: Houston, Texas

Services: Terminal, Network Connections, Personal IP, UUCP
Last Update: 2/24/94

Speedway Free Access

TEL: +1 503 520 2222
FAX: N/A
E-mail: info@speedway.net
Area Served: Most of U.S. plus International
Services: Terminal, Personal Information Services, Network Connections, UUCP
Last Update: 3/17/94

Sprint NSFNET ICM

Sprint NSFNET International Connections Manager
Attn: Robert Collet
TEL: +1 703 904 2230
E-mail: rcollet@icm1.icp.net
Area Served: International
Services: International network Connections to NSFNET; operates under cooperative agreement with NSF and conforms to CCIRN guidelines

SprintLink

13221 Woodland Park Road
Herndon, VA 22071
TEL: +1 800 877 7755
E-mail: info@sprintlink.net
Area Served: U.S. and International
Services: Network Connections

SUNET

UMDAC
S-901 87 Umea
SWEDEN
Attn: Hans Wallberg or Bjorn Eriksen
TEL: +46 90 16 56 45

FAX: +46 90 16 67 62
E-mail: postmaster@sunic.sunet.se
Area Served: Sweden

SURAnet Southeastern Universities Research Association Network

1353 Computer Science Center
University of Maryland
College Park, MD 20742-2411
Attn: Jack Hahn
TEL: +1 301 982 4600
E-mail: hahn@sura.net
Area Served: Southeastern U.S. (Alabama, Florida, Georgia, Kentucky, Louisiana, Mississippi, North Carolina, South Carolina, Tennessee, Virginia, and West Virginia)
Services: Network Connections

SURFnet

P.O. Box 19035
NL-3501 DA Utrecht
THE NETHERLANDS
TEL: +31 30310290
E-mail: info@surfnet.nl
c=nl, ADMD=400net, PRMD=SURF, O=SURFnet, S=info
Area served: The Netherlands

SwipNet AB

P.O. Box 62
S-164 94 KISTA
Sweden
TEL: +46 8-6324058
FAX: +46 8-6324200
E-mail: wallner@swip.net
Area Served: Sweden
Services: Terminal, UUCP
Last Update: 3/4/94

SWITCH

SWITCH Head Office
Limmatquai 138
CH-8001 Zurich
SWITZERLAND
TEL: +41 1 256 5454
FAX: +41 1 261 8133
E-mail: postmaster@switch.ch
C=CH;ADMD=arCom;PRMD=SWITCH;O=SWITCH; S=Postmaster;
Area Served: Switzerland

Systems Solutions (SSNet)

1254 Lorewood Grove Road
TEL: (302) 378-1386 (800) 331-1386
FAX: (302) 378-3871
E-mail: sharris@ssnet.com, info@ssnet.com
Area Served: Delaware (302 area code)
Services: Terminal, UUCP
Last Update: 3/17/94

TANet

Computer Center, Ministry of Education
12th Fl, No. 106
Sec. 2, Hoping E. Road
Taipei, Taiwan
Attn: Chen Wen-Sung
TEL: +886 2 7377010
FAX: +886 2 7377043
E-mail: nisc@twnmoe10.edu.tw
Area Served: Taiwan

TECHNET

National University of Singapore
10 Kent Ridge Crescent
SINGAPORE 0511
TEL: (65) 772-3119

E-mail: tommi@solomon.technet.sg
help@solomon.technet.sg
Area Served: Singapore (Acedemic and R&D Communities)
Services: Termainal, UUCP, Personal IP, Network Connections
Last Update: 4/5/94

TELEMEMO (Telecom Australia)

1/181 Victoria Parade
Collingwood
VICTORIA 3066
AUSTRALIA
TEL: +61 3 4121539/4121535/4121078
FAX: +61 3 4121548/4121545/6637941
E-mail: G=peter; S=kelleher; O=telecom; A=telememo;
C=au
Area Served: Australia
Services: X.400

Texas Metronet, Inc.

860 Kinwest Parkway (Suite 179)
Irving, TX 75063-3440
TEL: +1 214 705 2900
FAX: +1 214 401 2802
E-mail: info@metronet.com
Area Served: Terminal, UUCP, Personal IP
Last Update: 2/4/94

THEnet

Texas Higher Education Network
Computation Center
University of Texas
Austin, TX 78712
Attn: Tracy LaQuey Parker
TEL: +1 512 471 5046

E-mail: tracy@utexas.edu
Area Served: Texas
Services: Network Connections.

TICSA

The Internetworking Company of Southern Africa
P.O. Box 15525
Vlaeberg 8018
SOUTH AFRICA
TEL: +27 21 4192768
E-mail: info@ticsa.com
Area Served: Southern Africa
Services: Network Connections

TIPnet

Technical Sales and Support
Kjell Simenstad
MegaCom AB
Kjell Simenstad
121 80 Johanneshov
Stockholm
SWEDEN
TEL: +46 8 780 5616
FAX: +46 8 686 0213
Area Served: Sweden

TUVAKA

Ege Universitesi
Bilgisayar Arastirma ve Uygulama Merkezi
Bornova, Izmir 35100
TURKEY
Attn: Esra Delen
TEL: +90 51 887228
E-mail: Esra@ege.edu.tr
Esra@trearn.bitnet
Area Served: Turkey

UKnet

UKnet Support Group
Computing Laboratory
University of Kent
Canterbury
Kent CT2 7NF
UNITED KINGDOM
TEL: +44 227 475497, and +44 227 475415
FAX: +44 227 762811
E-mail: Postmaster@uknet.ac.uk
/S=postmaster/o=UKnet/PRMD=UK.AC
/ADMD=GOLD 400/C=GB/
Area Served: United Kingdom

UnBol/BolNet

Prof. Clifford Paravicini
Facultad de Ingenieria Electronica
Univ. Mayor de San Andres
La Paz
BOLIVA
E-mail: clifford@unbol.bo
Area Served: Bolivia

UNINETT

SINTEF DELAB
7034 Trondheim
NORWAY
Attn: Petter Kongshaug
TEL: +47 7 592980
E-mail: Petter.Kongshaug@delab.sintef.no
sekr@uninett.no
C=no; ADMD= ; PRMD=uninett; O=sintef;
OU=delab; S=kongshaug; G=petter;
Area Served: Norway

UNINET-ZA Project

Foundation for Research Development
P.O. Box 2600
Pretoria 0001
SOUTH AFRICA
Attn: Mr. Vic Shaw
TEL: +27 12 841 3542 or +27 12 841 2597
FAX: +27 12 804 2679   TELEX: 321312 SA
E-mail: uninet@frd.ac.za
Area Served: South Africa

University of Alaska Tundra Services

Tundra Services Coordinator
UAS Computing Services
11120 Glacier Highway
Juneau AK 99801
TEL: +1 907 465-6452
FAX: +1 907 465-6295
E-mail: JNJMB@acad1.alaska.edu
JXOPS@Tundra.alaska.edu
Area Served: State of Alaska (Public, Government,
Non-profits and the K-12 Education Community)
Services: Terminal
Last Update: 4/5/94

UUNET Canada Inc.

1 Yonge Street
Suite 1801
Toronto, Ontario
M5E 1W7
CANADA
TEL: +1 416 368 6621
FAX: +1 416 369 0515
E-mail: info@uunet.ca
Area Served: Canada
Services: Network Connections, Terminal, UUCP

UUNET India Limited
270N Road No. 10
Jubilee Hills
Hyderabad, A.P. 500 034 India
Attn: I Chandrashekar Rao or Narayan D Raju
TEL: +91 842 238007 or +91 842 247747
Fax : + 91 842 247787
E-mail: info@uunet.in
icr@uunet.in
ndr@uunet.in
Area Served: India
Services: Network Connections, Terminal, UUCP

UUNET Technologies, Inc.
3110 Fairview Park Drive
Suite 570
Falls Church, VA 22042
TEL: +1 800 488 6384 or +1 703 204 8000
FAX: 1 703 204 8001
E-mail: info@uunet.uu.net
Area Served: U.S., International
Services: Network Connections, Terminal, UUCP

UUNORTH
TEL: (416) 225-8649
FAX: (416) 225-0525
E-mail: uunorth@uunorth.north.net
Area Served: Canada and the Northern USA
Services: UUCP, Personal IP, Network Connection
Last Update: 4/5/94

VERnet
Virginia Education and Research Network
Academic Computing Center
Gilmer Hall
University of Virginia
Charlottesville, VA 22903
Attn: James Jokl

TEL: +1 804 924 0616
E-mail: jaj@virginia.edu
Area Served: Virginia
Services: Network Connections

VITA
Volunteers In Technical Assistance
1600 Wilson Boulevard 5th Floor
Arlington, VA 22209
USA
TEL: +1 703 276 1800
FAX: +1 703 243 1865 Telex: 440192 VITAUI
E-mail: vita@gmuvax.gmu.edu
Area Served: International
Services: Special—FTS (FidoNet) Polling Service,
Packet Radio, and Packet Satellite

Vnet Internet Access
P.O. Box 31474
Charlotte, NC 28231
USA
TEL: +1 800 377 3282
FAX: 704-334-6880
E-mail: info@vnet.net
Area Served: North Carolina (U.S. National access
also available via PDN.)
Services: Network Connections, Terminal, UUCP
Last Update: 2/16/94

WAMANI
CCI
Talcahuano 325-3F
1013 Buenos Aires
Argentina
TEL: +54 (1) 382-6842
E-mail: apoyo@wamani.apc.org
Area Served: Argentina
Services: Terminal, UUCP

Web

Nirv Centre
401 Richmond Street West
Suite 104
Toronto, Ontario M5V 3A8
CANADA
TEL: +1 (416) 596 0212
FAX: +1 (416) 974 9189
E-mail: support@web.apc.org
Area Served: International
Services: Terminal, UUCP

Westnet

Southwestern States Network
UCC
601 S. Howes, 6th Floor South
Colorado State University
Fort Collins, CO 80523
Attn: Pat Burns
TEL: +1 303 491 7260
E-mail: pburns@yuma.acns.colostate.edu
Area Served: Western U.S. (Arizona, Colorado, New Mexico, Utah, Idaho, and Wyoming)
Services: Network Connections

Whole Earth 'Lectronic Link (WELL)

27 Gate Five Road
Sausalito, CA 94965
TEL: +1 415 332 4335
E-mail: info@well.sf.ca.us
Area Served: San Francisco Bay Area
Services: Terminal

WIDE

c/o Prof. Jun Murai
KEIO University
5322 Endo, Fujisawa, 252

JAPAN
TEL: +81 466 47 5111 ext. 3330
E-mail: jun@wide.ad.jp
Area Served: Japan
Services: Terminal, UUCP

WiscNet

Madison Academic Computing Center
1210 W. Dayton Street
Madison, WI 53706
Attn: Tad Pinkerton
TEL: +1 608 262 8874
E-mail: tad@cs.wisc.edu
Area Served: Wisconsin
Services: Network Connections

The World

Software Tool & Die
1330 Beacon Street
Brookline, MA 02146
TEL: +1 617 739 0202
E-mail: office@world.std.com
Area Served: Boston (area code 617)
Services: Dialup Host, UUCP.

WVNET West Virginia Network for Educational Telecomputing

837 Chestnut Ridge Road
Morgantown, WV 26505
Attn: Harper Grimm
TEL: +1 304 293 5192
E-mail: cc011041@wvnvms.wvnet.edu
Area Served: West Virginia
Services: Network Connections

XMission

P.O. Box 510063
Salt Lake City, UT 84151-0063
USA
TEL: +1 801 539 0852
FAX: +1 801 539 0900
E-mail: support@xmission.com
Area Served: Utah
Services: Terminal, Network Connections, UUCP,
Business Services
Last Update: 2/4/94

XNet Information Systems

P.O. Box 1511
Lisle, IL 60532
USA
TEL: +1 708 983 6064
FAX: +1 708 983-6879
E-mail: admin@xnet.com
info@xnet.com
Area Served: Chicago, Illinois
Services: Terminal, UUCP
Last Update: 3/24/94

YUNAC

Borka Jerman-Blazic, Secretary General
Jamova 39
61000 Ljubljana
SLOVENIA
TEL: +38 61 159 199
FAX: +38 61 161 029
E-mail: jerman-blazic@ijs.ac.mail.yu
C=yu; ADMD=mail; PRMD=ac; O=ijs;
S=postmaster
Area Served: Slovenia, Croatia, Bosnia-Herzegovina

ZANGO

Zambia Association for Research and Development
Lusaka, Zambia
TEL: +260 1 252 507
Email: sysop@unza.gn.apc.org
Area Served: Zambia
Services: Terminal, UUCP

B

Guide to Client Applications

T his appendix contains a listing of the many client

applications available today as well as the appropri-

ate vendor information for each product. It has been

included to help guide your selection of client appli-

cations for your particular environment.

AIR NFS, AIR, AIR CORE, AIR SQL, AIR X, Internet in a Box, AIR Mail
Spry, Inc.
316 Occidental Avenue South, Suite 200
Seattle, WA 98104
VOICE: (800) 777-9638; (206) 447-0300
FAX: (206) 447-9008
E-mail: info@spry.com

Chameleon 4.0, Chameleon NFS 4.0, Chameleon 32 4.0 (NT), Chameleon 32 NFS 4.0, Chameleon X 4.0, Chameleon D 4.0, Chameleon NFS/D 4.0, Internet Chameleon
NetManage, Inc.
10725 North De Anza Boulevard
Cupertino, CA 95014
VOICE: (408) 973-7171
FAX: (408) 257-6405
E-mail: info@netmanage.com

Cyberdesk 2.0
CyberCorp, Inc.
P.O. Drawer 1988
Kennesay, GA 30144
TEL: (404) 424-6240
FAX: (404) 424-8995

ECSMail 3.0, ECSMail for Windows
Isa Corp.
10040 104th Street, Suite 835
Edmonton, Alberta, Canada T5J0Z2
TEL: (403) 420-8081
FAX: (403) 420-8037
Tech support: (403) 420-7760

E-Mail Connection 3.0, Internet Connection 1.0
ConnectSoft
11130 NE 33rd Place, Suite 250
Bellevue, WA 98004-1448
TEL: (800) 234-9497; (206) 827-6467
FAX: (206) 822-9095

EMBLA 1.1
ICL Enterprises, NA
11490 Commerce Park Drive
Reston, VA 22091
TEL: (703) 648-3380

Eudora 2.1, Eudora for Windows 2.1
Qualcomm, Inc.
6455 Lusk Boulevard
San Diego, CA 92121-2799
TEL: (800) 238-3672; (619) 587-1121
FAX: (619) 597-5058

EXceed 4.0
Hummingbird Communications LTD
2900 John Street
Markham, Ontario, Canada L3R 5G3
VOICE: (905) 470-1203
FAX: (905) 470-1207
E-mail: support@hcl.com

HoloGate
Information Access Technologies, Inc.
46 Shattuck Square, Suite 11
Berkeley, CA 94704-1152
TEL: (510) 704-0160
FAX: (510) 704-8019
Tech support BBS: (800) NET-HOLO

IMail 1.0

Ipswitch, Inc.
669 Main Street
Wakefield, MA 01880
TEL: (617) 246-1150
FAX: (617) 245-2975

InterMail

SecureWare, Inc.
2957 Clairmont Road, Suite 200
Atlanta, GA 30329-1647
TEL: (404) 315-0293

Ishmail

HaL Software Systems
3006A Longhome Boulevard, Suite 113
Austin, Texas 78758
TEL: (800) 762-0253; (512) 834-9962
FAX: (512) 834-9963

LAN Workgroup 4.12, LAN WorkPlace for DOS 4.12

Novell Inc.
2180 Fortune Drive
San Jose, CA 95131
VOICE: (800) 243-8526; (801) 429-7000
E-mail: info@novell.com

Lotus cc:Mail Desktop for Unix 1.1

Lotus Development Corp.
800 El Camino Real, W
Mountain View, CA 94040
TEL: (800) 448-2500; (415) 961-8800
FAX: (415) 961-0840
Tech support: (415) 966-4900
Tech support BBS: (415) 691-0128

Mail*Link Internet for PowerTalk 1.5, MailSTAR

StarNine TEchnologies, Inc.
2550 Ninth Street, Suite 112
Berkeley, CA 94710-2204
TEL: (510) 649-4949
FAX: (510) 548-0393

Major Gateway/Internet

Galacticomm, Inc.
4101 SW 47th Avenue, Suite 101
Ft. Lauderdale, FL 33314
TEL: (800) 328-1128; (305) 583-5990
FAX: (305) 583-7846
Tech support: (305) 321-2404
Tech support BBS: (305) 583-7808

Microsoft Exchange Server

Microsoft Corp.
One Microsoft Way
Redmond, WA 98052-6399
TEL: (800) 426-9400; (206) 882-8080
Direct sales: (800) MSPRESS
FAX: (206) 635-6100
Tech support: (206) 454-2030;
(206) 637-7098 (Windows)
Tech support BBS: (206) 936-6735

MKS Internet Anywhere

MKS
35 King Street North
Waterloo, Ontario, Canada N2N 2W9
VOICE: (800) 265-2797; (519) 884-2251
FAX: (519) 884-8861
E-mail: inquiry@mks.com

NetCruiser/NetCruiserPLUS 2.0

NETCOM On-Line Communications Services, Inc.
3031 Tisch Way, 2nd Floor
San Jose, CA 95128
VOICE: (800) 353-6600; (408) 345-2600
FAX: (408) 241-9145

PC-NFS 5.1

SunSoft
Two Elizabeth Drive
Chelmsford, MA 01824
Voice: (508) 442-2300
FAX: (508) 250-2300

PC/TCP for DOS and Windows

FTP Software, Inc.
100 Brickstone Square
North Andover, MA 01810
VOICE: (800) 282-4387; (508) 685-4000
FAX: (508) 794-4477
E-mail: info@ftp.com

Pronto: Remote Windows to Unix E-mail 1.5, Pronto/IP

CommTouch Software, Inc.
1206 W. Hillsdale Boulevard, Suite C
San Mateo, CA 94403
VOICE: (800) 638-6824; (415) 578-6580
FAX: (415) 578-8580

QM-Postman 1.3

Netstrategy, Inc.
1071 King Street, W, Suite 418
Toronto, Ontario, Canada M6K 3K2
TEL: (416) 345-8985
FAX: (416) 345-9044

QuickMail Internet Access Kit 1.5, QuickMail Internet Access Kit 1.5 for Windows

CE Software, Inc.
P.O. Box 65580, 1801 Industrial Circle
West Des Moines, IA 50265-6558
TEL: (800) 523-7638; (515) 221-1801
FAX: (515) 221-1803
Tech Support: (515) 221-1803

SirenMail 2.0, SirenMail 2.0 for Windows

Siren Software Corp.
505 Hamilton Avenue, Suite 100
Palo Alto, CA 94301
TEL: (800) 457-4736; (415) 322-0600
FAX: (415) 322-9999

Special Delivery

Expaand Technology Corp.
24285 Sunnymead Boulevard, Suite 286
Moreno Valley, CA 92553
TEL: (800) 397-2263; (909) 242-6250
FAX: (909) 924-7061

SuperTCP 4.0, SuperTCP NFS 4.0

Frontier Technologies
10201 North Port Washington Road
Mequon, WI 53092
VOICE: (414) 241-4555
FAX: (414) 241-7084
E-mail: tcp@frontiertech.com

UUCP/Connect Server, UUCP/Connect Client

InterCon Systems Corporation
950 Herndon Parkway, Suite 420
Herndon, VA 22070
VOICE: (703) 709-9890
FAX: (703) 709-5555
E-mail: comment@intercon.com

UULINK

Vortex Technology
23241 Ventura Boulevard, Suite 208
Woodland Hills, CA 91364
VOICE: (818) 225-2800
FAX: (818) 225-7203
E-mail: sales@vortex.com

UUPlus

UUPlus
P.O. Box 8
Camarillo, CA 93011
VOICE: (805) 485-0057
E-mail: info@uuplus.com

WinGopher, WinGopher Complete

Ameritech Library Services (Academic Division)
1007 Church Street
Evanston, IL 60201-3622
VOICE: (800) 556-6847; (708) 866-4944
FAX: (708) 866-4893

Z-Mail 3.2.1

Network Computing Devices, Inc.
101 Rowland Way, Suite 300
Novato, CA 94945
TEL: (415) 898-8649
FAX: (415) 898-8299

Registering Your Site

This appendix contains an exact copy of the Domain Name Form as presented in the InterNIC. Anyone seeking to register for an Internet domain name must obtain and complete this form. Use this copy, however, only as a guide to the types of questions asked. Because it is constantly being updated, obtain the actual form from the InterNIC once you are ready to register.

Domain Name Form from InterNIC

Be advised in order to register for a domain name you must have at least an active primary and secondary name server up and running on the Internet. If you do not you will need to go through a service provider whereby you may obtain some level of service where they would allow you to use their name servers until you have established your own. After you have established your own, you may update your domain record to reflect your own name servers.

Hostmaster: InterNIC Registration Services

`<templates/domain-templates.txt>`   [07/94]

To establish a domain, the following information must be sent to the InterNIC Registration Services (HOSTMASTER@INTERNIC.NET). Either this template, or the "short form" following this template may be used.

(1) The name of the top-level domain to join (EDU, GOV, COM, NET, ORG).

1. Top-level domain:

(2) The name of the domain (up to 24 characters). This is the name that will be used in tables and lists associating the domain with the domain servers addresses. While domain names can be quite long, the use of shorter, more user-friendly names is recommended.

2. Complete Domain Name:

(3) The name and address of the organization for which the domain is being established.

3a. Organization name:

3b. Organization address:

(4) The date you expect the domain to be fully operational.

4. Date operational:

 The key people must have electronic mailboxes (even if in the domain being registered) and "handles" (unique InterNIC database identifiers). If you have access to "WHOIS", please check to see if the contacts are registered and if so, include only the handle and changes (if any) that need to be made in the entry. If you do not have access to "WHOIS", please provide all the information indicated and a handle will be assigned.

(5) The handle of the administrative head of the organization in (3) above or this person's name, postal address, phone number, organization, and network emailbox. This is the contact point for administrative and policy questions about the domain.

Administrative Contact
5a. Handle (if known):

b. Name (Last, First):

5c. Organization:

5d. Postal Address:

5e. Phone Number:

5f. Net Mailbox:

(6) The handle of the technical contact for the domain or this person's name, mailing address, phone number, organization, and network mailbox. This is the contact point for problems and updates regarding the domain or zone.

Technical and Zone Contact

6a. Handle (if known):

6b. Name (Last, First):

6c. Organization:

6d. Postal Address:

6e. Phone Number:

6f. Net Mailbox:

 Domains must provide at least two independent servers for translating names to addresses for hosts in the domain. The servers should be in physically separate locations and on different networks if possible. The servers should be active and responsive to DNS queries BEFORE this application is submitted. Incomplete information in sections 7 and 8 or inactive servers will result in delay of the registration.

(7) The primary server information.

7a. Primary Server Hostname:

7b. Primary Server Netaddress:

7c. Primary Server Hardware:

7d. Primary Server Software:

(8) The secondary server information.

8a. Secondary Server Hostname:

8b. Secondary Server Netaddress:

8c. Secondary Server Hardware:

8d. Secondary Server Software:

(9) Please briefly describe the organization for which this domain is being registered. If the domain is for an organization that already has a domain registered, please describe the purpose of this domain.

For further information contact InterNIC Registration Services:

> Via electronic mail:
> HOSTMASTER@INTERNIC.NET
>
> Via telephone: (703) 742-4777
>
> Via facsimile: (703) 742-4811
>
> Via postal mail: Network Solutions
>
> InterNIC Registration Services
>
> 505 Huntmar Park Drive
>
> Herndon, VA 22070

The party requesting registration of this name certifies that, to her/his knowledge, the use of this name does not violate trademark or other statues.

Registering a domain name does not confer any legal rights to that name and any disputes between parties over the rights to use a particular name are to be settled between the contending parties using normal legal methods.

(See RFC 1591)

1. Top-level domain:

2. Complete Domain Name:

3a. Organization name:

3b. Organization address:

4. Operational Date:

Administrative Contact

5a. NIC Handle (if known):

5b. Name (Last, First):

5c. Organization:

5d. Postal Address:

5e. Phone Number:

5f. Net Mailbox:

Technical/Zone Contact

6a. NIC Handle (if known):

6b. Name (Last, First):

6c. Organization:

6d. Postal Address:

6e. Phone Number:

6f. Net Mailbox:

7a. Prime Server Hostname:

7b. Prime Server Netaddress:

7c. Prime Server Hardware:

7d. Prime Server Software:

8a. Second Server Hostname:

8b. Second Server Netaddress:

8c. Second Server Hardware:

8d. Second Server Software:

9. Domain/Org Purpose/Desc.:

 In Sections 3b, 5d, & 6d use multiple lines for addresses. If contacts are registered, only 5a and 6a are needed. If servers are registered, only 7a&b and 8a&b are needed. If there is more than one secondary server, just copy Section 8.

The party requesting registration of this name certifies that, to her/his knowledge, the use of this name does not violate trademark or other statutes.

Registering a domain name does not confer any legal rights to that name and any disputes between parties over the rights to use a particular name are to be settled between the contending parties using normal legal methods.

(See RFC 1591)

IP Address Form

Following is the form for applying for an IP address. It is an actual email interaction with the InterNIC.

Please first contact the Internet Service Provider (ISP) of your choice to obtain an IP number, if you plan on connecting to the Internet as soon as possible. We have allocated blocks of numbers out to them for this purpose.

However, if, you do not plan on connecting to the internet right away you may complete the enclosed internet-number-template.txt. However, under section 1 of the enclosed IP template, please incorporate a "note" indicating your estimated date of connecting to the internet. Please be advised that your application will be returned if you do not indicate the date you plan to connect to the internet.

Hostmaster: InterNic Registration Services

[templates/internet-number-template.txt]
[09/94]

This form must be completed as part of the application process for obtaining an Internet Protocol (IP) Network Number. To obtain an Internet number, please provide the following information on-line, via electronic mail, to HOSTMASTER@INTERNIC.NET. If electronic mail is not available to you, please mail hardcopy to:

Network Solutions

InterNIC Registration Services

505 Huntmar Park Drive

Herndon, VA 22070

FAX to (703) 742-4811

Once Registration Services receives your completed application we will send you an acknowledgement, via electronic or postal mail.

 This application is solely for obtaining a legitimate IP network number assignment. If you're interested in officially registering a domain please complete the domain application found in templates/domain-template.txt. If FTP is not available to you, please contact HOSTMASTER@INTERNIC.NET or phone the NIC at (703) 742-4777 for further assistance.

 1. European network requests should use the european template (templates/european-ip template.txt). Please follow their instructions for submission.

2. Networks that will be connected/located within the geographic region maintained by the Asian-Pacific NIC should use the APNIC template (templates/apnic-001.txt). Please follow their instructions for submission.

Non-Connected Networks

If the networks you are requesting address space for will never to be connected to the Internet, you are required to refer to and adhere to the guidelines set forth in RFC 1597, under section 3 "private address space." This RFC contains important information regarding the Policies/Procedures that are to be implemented when IP address space is requested for networks that will NEVER be connected to the Internet. A large portion of address space (one (1) class A, sixteen (16) class Bs and two-hundred fifty-six (256) class Cs) has been reserved for address allocation for non-connected networks. Please obtain the IP address space you require by utilizing the IP address range(s) that have been reserved by the IANA for use by all non-connected networks specified in this RFC. RFC 1597 may be obtained via anonymous FTP from DS.INTERNIC.NET (198.49.45.10).

 Your application must be typed.

Connected Networks

(1) If the network will be connected to the Internet, you must provide the name of the governmental sponsoring organization or commercial service provider, and the name, title, mailing address, phone number, net mailbox, and NIC Handle (if any) of the contact person (POC) at that organization who has authorized the network connection. This person will serve as the POC for administrative and policy questions about authorization to be a part of the Internet. Examples of such sponsoring organizations are: DISA DNS, The National Science Foundation (NSF), or similar government, educational or commercial network service providers.

 If the network will never be connected to the internet, please utilize the address space reserved for non-connected networks that is specified in RFC 1597. If you intend to connect this network to the Internet but have not yet chosen a service provider, leave this section blank, but indicate the approximate date of your internet connection in section 9 of this template. If you intend to connect to the internet and have already chosen a provider, you are required to submit this request to your service provider for processing. Service providers are allocated blocks of addresses to support the networking needs of their customers. This procedure will ensure that the number of entries added to the internet routing tables is kept to a minimum, and cidr is used as efficiently as possible. The above procedures pertain exclusively to requests for class C address(es).

1a. Sponsoring Organization:

1b. Contact name (Lastname, Firstname):

1c. Contact title:

1d. Mail Address :

1e. Phone:

1f. Net mailbox:

1g. NIC handle (if known):

(2) Provide the name, title, mailing address, phone number, and organization of the technical Point-of-Contact (POC). The on-line mailbox and NIC Handle (if any) of the technical POC should also be included. This is the POC for resolving technical problems associated with the network and for updating information about the network. The technical POC may also be responsible for hosts attached to this network.

2a. NIC handle (if known):

2b. Technical POC name (Lastname, Firstname):

2c. Technical POC title:

2d. Mail address:

2e. Phone:

2f. Net Mailbox:

(3) Supply the SHORT mnemonic name for the network (up to 12 characters). This is the name that will be used as an identifier in internet name and address tables. The only special character that may be used in a network name is a dash (-). Please do not use periods or underscores. The syntax XXXX.com and XXXX.net are not valid network naming conventions and should only be used when applying for a domain.

3. Network name:

(4) Identify the geographic location of the network and the organization responsible for establishing the network.

4a. Postal address for main/headquarters network site:

4b. Name of Organization:

(5) Question #5 is for military or DoD requests, only.

If you require that this connected network be announced to the NSFNET please answer questions 5a, 5b, and 5c. If this network will be connected to the Internet via MILNET, this application must be submitted to HOSTMASTER@NIC.DDN.MIL for review/processing.

5a. Do you want MILNET to announce your network to the NSFNET? (Y/N):

5b. Do you have an alternate connection, other than MILNET, to the NSFNET?   (please state alternate connection if answer is yes):

5c. If you've answered yes to 5b, please state if you would like the MILNET connection to act as a backup path to the NSFNET? (Y/N):

(6) Estimate the size of the network to include the number of hosts and subnets/segments that will be supported by the network. A "host" is defined as any device (PC, printer etc.) that will be assigned an address from the host portion of the network number. A host may also be characterized as a node or device.

Host Information

6a. Initially:

6b. Within one year:

6c. Within two years:

6d. Within five years:

Subnet/Segment Information

6e. Initially:

6f. Within one year:

6g. Within two years:

6h. Within five years:

(7) Unless a strong and convincing reason is presented, the network (if it qualifies at all) will be assigned a single class C network number. If a class C network number is not acceptable for your purposes, you are required to submit substantial, detailed justification in support of your requirements.

 The NIC would strongly suggest you consider subnetting class C addresses when multiple segments will be used to support a minimal amount of host addresses. Multiple class C numbers should be utilized when it is necessary to support more than 256 hosts on a single network. You may wish to confer with a network consultant and router vendor for additional information.

 If there are plans for more than a few local networks, and more than 100 hosts, you are strongly urged to consider subnetting.

[Reference RFC 950 and RFC 1466]

7. Reason:

(8) Networks are characterized as being either Research, Educational, Government—Non Defense, or Commercial, and the network address space is shared between these four areas. Which type is this network?

8. Type of network:

(9) What is the purpose of the network?

9. Purpose:

For further information contact InterNIC Registration Services:

>Via electronic mail:
>HOSTMASTER@INTERNIC.NET

>Via telephone: (703) 742-4777

>Via postal mail: Network Solutions

>InterNIC Registration Service

>505 Huntmar Park Drive

>Herndon, VA 22070

Recommended Reading

The information in the following list is available through anonymous FTP from DS.INTERNIC.NET (198.49.45.10); or you can call 1-619-455-4600.

Gerich, E., Guidelines for Management of IP Address Space, Ann Arbor, I: Merit Network, Inc.; May 1993; RFC 1466. 10 p. (DS.INTERNIC.NET RFC1466.TXT).

Rekhter, Y., Moskowitz. B., Karrenberg, D., de Groot, G. Address Allocation for Private Internets, IBM Corp., Chrysler Corp., RIPE NCC; March 1994; RFC 1597. 8 p. (DS.INTERNIC.NET RFC1597.TXT).

Braden, R.T.; Postel, J.B. Requirements for Internet Gateways. Marina del Rey, CA: University of Southern California, Information Sciences Inst.; 1987 June; RFC 1009. 55 p. (DS.INTERNET.NET POLICY FC1009.TXT).

Internet Engineering Task Force, Braden, R.T. Requirements for nternet Hosts—Communication Layers. Marina del Rey, CA: University of Southern California, Information Sciences Inst.; October 1989; RFC 1122. 116 p. (DS.INTERNIC.NET RFC1122.TXT).

Internet Engineering Task Force, Braden, R.T. Requirements for Internet Hosts—Application and Support. Marina del Rey, CA: University of Southern California, Information Sciences Inst.; October 1989; RFC 1123. 98 p. (DS.INTERNIC.NET RFC1123.TXT).

Internet Activities Board. Internet Official Protocol Standards. 1994 March; RFC 1600. 34p. (DS.INTERNIC.NET POLICY RFC1600.TXT). [The current version is always available as "STD 1".]

Mogul, J.; Postel, J.B. Internet Standard Subnetting Procedure. Stanford, CA: Stanford University; 1985 August; RFC 950. 18 p. (DS.INTERNIC.NET POLICY RFC950.TXT).

Postel, J.B. Internet Control Message Protocol. Marina del Rey, CA: University of Southern California, Information Sciences Inst.; 1981 September; RFC 792. 21 p. (DS.INTERNIC.NET POLICY RFC792.TXT).

Postel, J.B. Transmission Control Protocol. Marina del Rey, CA: University of Southern California, Information Sciences Inst.; 1981 September; RFC 793. 85 p. (DS.INTERNIC.NET POLICY RFC793.TXT).

Postel, J.B. Address Mappings. Marina del Rey, CA: University of Southern California, Information Sciences Inst.; 1981 September; RFC 796. 7 p. (DS.INTERNIC.NET POLICY RFC796.TXT). Obsoletes: IEN 115 (NACC 0968-79).

Postel, J.B. User Datagram Protocol. Marina del Rey, CA: University of Southern California, Information Sciences Inst.; 1980 August 28; RFC 768. 3 p. (DS.INTERNIC.NET POLICY RFC768.TXT).

Postel, J.B. Internet Protocol. Marina del Rey, CA: University of Southern California, Information Sciences Inst.; 1981 September; RFC 791. 45 p. (DS.INTERNIC.NET POLICY RFC791.TXT).

Reynolds, J.K.; Postel, J.B. Assigned Numbers. Marina del Rey, CA: University of Southern California, Information Sciences Inst.; 1992 July; RFC 1340. 139p. (DS.INTERNIC.NET POLICY RFC1340.TXT). The current version is always available as "STD 2".

B

E

F

fallback (modems), 40
File Transfer Protocol (FTP), 71
Fnet Sylvain Langlois (provider), 163
forms
    Domain Name Form, 196-198
    IP address applications, 198-199
Frame Relay (packet switching), 47-49
    accessing, 49
    CIR (Committed Information Rate), 48-49
    costs, 49
    PVCs (Permanent Virtual Circuits), 48
    WANs, 143
Freelance Systems Programming
    (provider), 163
FTP (File Transfer Protocol), 110-111
    anonymous, 111
    servers, 88-90, 138
        anonymous connections, 89
        configuring, 89-90
        help, 90
        security, 88-90
    TCP/IP, 71
Full Access (server security), 133-135
FUNET (Finnish University and Research
    Network), 163

G

GARR (Gruppo Armonizzazione delle Reti per
    la Ricerca), 164
GBnet (provider), 164
GEONET (provider), 164
GLAIDS Internet BBS (provider), 164
GlasNet (provider), 164

Global Enterprise Service, Inc. (provider), 164
GLUK—GlasNet-Ukraine, Ltd (provider), 164
gnu (classification), 108
Gopher, 112-113
    servers, 96-99, 139-140
        cache files, 99
        directories, 98
        installing, 97-98
        log files, 99
        system requirements, 97
        type mappings, 99
        uninstalling, 98
        Unix, 99
GreenNet (provider), 164
growth (Internet), 6

H

Halcyon (provider), 165
hardware connections
    dial-up services, 114-115
    ISDN, 114-115
    routers, 115
HEANET (provider), 165
help (FTP servers), 90
hep (classification), 108
history of Internet, 20-22
HISTRIA (ABM-BBS) (provider), 165
hobbies (servers), 108
HoloGate (client application), 190
HoloNet (provider), 165
home pages (WWW), 91
    business, 91-92
home site (providers), 150
Hong Kong Supernet (provider), 165
HookUp Communications (provider), 165

J

X-Y-Z

WANT MORE INFORMATION?

CHECK OUT THESE RELATED TOPICS OR SEE YOUR LOCAL BOOKSTORE

CAD and 3D Studio

As the number one CAD publisher in the world, and as a Registered Publisher of Autodesk, New Riders Publishing provides unequaled content on this complex topic. Industry-leading products include AutoCAD and 3D Studio.

Networking

As the leading Novell NetWare publisher, New Riders Publishing delivers cutting-edge products for network professionals. We publish books for all levels of users, from those wanting to gain NetWare Certification, to those administering or installing a network. Leading books in this category include *Inside NetWare 3.12*, *CNE Training Guide: Managing NetWare Systems*, *Inside TCP/IP*, and *NetWare: The Professional Reference*.

Graphics

New Riders provides readers with the most comprehensive product tutorials and references available for the graphics market. Best-sellers include *Inside CorelDRAW! 5*, *Inside Photoshop 3*, and *Adobe Photoshop NOW!*

Internet and Communications

As one of the fastest growing publishers in the communications market, New Riders provides unparalleled information and detail on this ever-changing topic area. We publish international best-sellers such as *New Riders' Official Internet Yellow Pages, 2nd Edition*, a directory of over 10,000 listings of Internet sites and resources from around the world, and *Riding the Internet Highway, Deluxe Edition*.

Operating Systems

Expanding off our expertise in technical markets, and driven by the needs of the computing and business professional, New Riders offers comprehensive references for experienced and advanced users of today's most popular operating systems, including *Understanding Windows 95*, *Inside Unix*, *Inside Windows 3.11 Platinum Edition*, *Inside OS/2 Warp Version 3*, and *Inside MS-DOS 6.22*.

Other Markets

Professionals looking to increase productivity and maximize the potential of their software and hardware should spend time discovering our line of products for Word, Excel, and Lotus 1-2-3. These titles include *Inside Word 6 for Windows*, *Inside Excel 5 for Windows*, *Inside 1-2-3 Release 5*, and *Inside WordPerfect for Windows*.

Orders/Customer Service   **1-800-653-6156**   Source Code   **NRP95**

New Riders Publishing   201 West 103rd Street ◆ Indianapolis, Indiana 46290 USA

Name _____ Title _____

Company_____ Type of
business _____

Address _____

City/State/ZIP _____

Have you used these types of books before?　☐ yes　　☐ no

If yes, which ones? _____

_____

How many computer books do you purchase each year?　☐ 1–5　　☐ 6 or more

How did you learn about this book? _____

Where did you purchase this book? _____

Which applications do you currently use? _____

_____

Which computer magazines do you subscribe to? _____

_____

What trade shows do you attend? _____

_____

Comments: _____

_____

_____

Would you like to be placed on our preferred mailing list?　☐ yes　　☐ no

☐ **I would like to see my name in print!** You may use my name and quote me in future New Riders products and promotions. My daytime phone number is: _____

New Riders Publishing　201 West 103rd Street ◆ Indianapolis, Indiana 46290　USA

Fax to ` 317-581-4670 `　　Orders/Customer Service ` 1-800-653-6156 `　　Source Code ` NRP95 `

Fold Here

NO POSTAGE
NECESSARY
IF MAILED
IN THE
UNITED STATES

BUSINESS REPLY MAIL

FIRST-CLASS MAIL PERMIT NO. 9918 INDIANAPOLIS IN

POSTAGE WILL BE PAID BY THE ADDRESSEE

**NEW RIDERS PUBLISHING
201 W 103RD ST
INDIANAPOLIS IN 46290-9058**